THE DOPAMINE CARTEL

Unmasking the Lethal Trap of the Social Media Matrix

Table of Contents

INTRODUCTION

You don't remember deciding to pick it up. One moment you are waking up, your eyes barely adjusted to the morning light, and the next, your thumb is already in motion. Swipe, scroll, tap. A rush of breaking news, curated lifestyles, fleeting outrage, and bite-sized entertainment floods your brain before your feet have even touched the floor. This is not an accident. It is not a lack of personal willpower or a moral failing on your part. It is the flawless execution of a trillion-dollar business model.

Welcome to the Social Media Matrix.

For over a decade, we have been told that social media platforms are neutral public squares—digital town halls designed to connect humanity, share ideas, and build communities. But behind the glossy interfaces and corporate mission statements about "bringing the world closer together," a very different reality exists. At the highest echelons of the tech industry, a sophisticated syndicate of data scientists, behavioral psychologists, and algorithmic engineers has quietly built the most effective system of human behavioral modification in history.

This is the Dopamine Cartel.

Unlike traditional cartels that traffic in illicit substances, this syndicate trades in something far more intimate and vastly more profitable: your human attention. They have weaponized our fundamental biological need for connection, validation, and information, turning our own neurochemistry against us. By exploiting the brain's dopamine reward pathways through intermittent variable rewards—the exact same psychological mechanism used in casino slot machines—they have ensured that we can never simply log off. We are neurologically compelled to stay, to scroll, to react, and to consume.

The Matrix they have built is an invisible architecture that surrounds our daily lives. It subtly dictates what we buy, who we trust, how we perceive our bodies, and how we measure our self-worth. Inside the Matrix, outrage is prioritized over nuance because anger keeps eyes on the screen. Comparison is amplified over contentment because insecurity drives frantic consumption. Deep, sustained focus is shattered into fragmented seconds of attention, leaving us exhausted, anxious, and profoundly isolated despite being more "connected" than any generation before us.

The Dopamine Cartel: Unmasking the Lethal Trap of the Social Media Matrix is not a manifesto against technology itself. Technology, in its purest form, is a tool. This book is an investigation into the deliberate, malicious manipulation of that tool. It is an exposé of how the attention economy harvests human experience as raw material, repackaging our habits and vulnerabilities into behavioral data sold to the highest bidder.

Over the course of this book, we will dismantle the Matrix piece by piece. We will explore the dark science of digital addiction, examine the architects who built the cage, and uncover the devastating toll this constant connectivity is taking on our mental health, our youth, and our social fabric.

But more importantly, this book is a blueprint for escape.

Understanding the trap is the first and most crucial step toward dismantling it. You cannot break free from a prison if you do not recognize the bars. By shining a harsh light on the psychological triggers and algorithmic manipulation designed to keep you compliant, you can begin to reclaim your autonomy. You can rebuild your attention span, rediscover the rich depth of the physical world, and establish boundaries that protect your peace of mind.

The Cartel relies entirely on your passive, continuous participation. It requires your absolute distraction. It is time to wake up, see the code for exactly what it is, and take your mind back.

CHAPTER 1:
THE ARCHITECTURE OF ADDICTION

Welcome to the foundation of the Matrix. If you want to understand how a trap works, you must first study its architecture. Chapter 1 strips away the user-friendly interfaces, the colorful app icons, and the harmless notifications to reveal the stark, calculating machinery operating beneath the glass of your screen.

We often blame ourselves for our inability to put our phones down. We label it a lack of discipline, a fleeting attention span, or a modern bad habit. But the truth is far more clinical and unsettling: your brain is simply doing exactly what it evolved to do, and the architects of the social media ecosystem know this better than anyone. They have not merely built platforms for digital communication; they have successfully reverse-engineered the human nervous system.

In this chapter, we will explore the meticulously designed **Architecture of Addiction**. We will begin by demystifying the biological driver of all human motivation—dopamine—and examine how tech giants have hijacked this ancient survival mechanism to keep you perpetually scrolling. You will discover how the principles of behavioral psychology, initially observed in animal laboratories and perfected on casino floors, were seamlessly integrated into your daily digital routine through intermittent variable rewards. Every swipe to refresh, every unexpected ping, and every glowing red notification badge is a calculated pull of a digital slot machine lever.

Finally, we will follow the money to understand the *why*. Why go to such extreme, manipulative lengths to capture your waking hours? The answer lies in the Attention Economy, a ruthless financial system where your focus is the ultimate currency. By the end of this chapter, the illusion of "free" digital services will shatter, replaced by the concrete understanding that when you do not pay for the product, your mind is the product.

1.1 The Science of the Scroll: How Digital Dopamine Works

We must first dismantle a popular myth. For years, pop psychology has labeled dopamine as the "pleasure chemical." We are told that dopamine is the warm, satisfying feeling we get when we eat a delicious meal, win a game, or receive a compliment. Neuroscientists know this definition is dangerously incomplete. Dopamine is not about the *experience* of pleasure; it is about the *anticipation* of it. It is the neurochemical driver of motivation, craving, and pursuit. Dopamine does not say, "This feels good." It says, "That looks good. Go get it, and do not stop until you have it."

Millions of years ago, this relentless biological engine kept our ancestors alive. In a harsh, unpredictable environment where food and resources were scarce, dopamine was the ultimate survival mechanism. It compelled early humans to keep walking over the next hill, to forage under one more rock, and to seek out new information. When you found a berry bush, dopamine rewarded your brain, hardwiring the behavior so you would do it again. The system was perfectly calibrated for a world of scarcity. Today, however, our brains are operating on that exact same ancient hardware, but we are navigating an environment of unnatural, infinite abundance.

Enter the "infinite scroll," a design feature so ubiquitous today that it feels like a natural law of the internet. But it was not an accident. Invented in 2006, the infinite scroll eliminated a crucial, naturally occurring element in human behavior: the stopping cue. In the physical world, things end. A book has chapters. A newspaper has a final page. A television show rolls its credits. These stopping cues offer our brains a moment of pause, a subconscious opportunity to ask, "Do I want to continue doing this, or should I move on to something else?" The infinite scroll brutally removed the bottom of the page, stripping away your brain's natural off-ramp.

When you drag your thumb up your smartphone, you initiate a highly engineered neurochemical loop. Here is what happens:

- **The Cue:** You feel a micro-pang of boredom, anxiety, or simply the muscle memory of holding your device.
- **The Craving:** Your brain anticipates a reward—a funny video, a validating "like," or breaking news. Dopamine floods your system, compelling action.
- **The Response:** You swipe. The physical friction to act is essentially zero.
- **The Reward:** The screen renders a new piece of content to consume.

Crucially, the digital reward rarely matches the intensity of the initial craving. The content is often mildly amusing at best, or actively infuriating at worst. But because the anticipation was so high, the brain immediately seeks to resolve the deficit. So, you swipe again. And again. You are not scrolling because you are finding deep, lasting satisfaction; you are scrolling because your dopamine circuitry demands that you keep foraging. You are digging for digital berries in a bottomless bucket. Over time, your brain adapts to this constant hyper-stimulation by down-regulating its natural dopamine receptors. Your neurological baseline shifts. Activities that used to bring you quiet joy—reading a physical book, having a slow conversation, or simply staring out a window—suddenly feel agonizingly dull. You now require more intense, rapid fire stimulation just to feel a baseline level of normal.

The architects of the Social Media Matrix understand this biological vulnerability intimately. They know that if they can keep you in a state of perpetual anticipation, they can seamlessly bypass your rational decision-making centers. Your prefrontal cortex—the specialized part of the brain responsible for long-term planning, impulse control, and critical thinking—is effectively subdued by the sheer volume of dopamine demanding immediate satisfaction. You become a passive participant in your own life, temporarily paralyzed by the glow of a glass rectangle.

As users, we are not simply fighting a personal lack of willpower or a character flaw; we are actively fighting a ruthless, trillion-dollar industry that has successfully placed a direct IV line right into our neural pathways. The modern science of the scroll is fundamentally the science of exploitation. But fully understanding this mechanism is the first step toward reclaiming your agency. Once you see the infinite scroll not as a modern convenience, but as a deliberate neurological hack, its power begins to fracture. The vital question then becomes for the user: precisely how do they ensure that these psychological rewards are just unpredictable enough to keep the dopamine flowing endlessly?

1.2 Intermittent Variable Rewards: The Slot Machine in Your Pocket

If you walk into any major casino, you will immediately notice the atmosphere. There are no clocks on the walls, no windows to indicate the passing of the sun, and a cacophony of carefully engineered sights and sounds designed to keep you seated. But the true star of the casino floor is the slot machine. It is the most profitable device in the gambling industry, not because the payouts are large, but because the psychological hook is inescapable. Now, reach into your pocket. You are carrying a miniaturized version of that exact same machine, operating on the precise same psychological principles.

To understand how your smartphone became a digital slot machine, we must look back to the mid-twentieth century and behavioral psychologist B.F. Skinner. Skinner is famous for his experiments using the "Skinner Box," a controlled environment where animals, typically pigeons, were tested to see how behaviors could be shaped by rewards. Initially, Skinner set up the box so that every time a pigeon pecked a specific lever, it received a food pellet. The pigeons quickly learned the connection. Peck the lever, get the food. This continuous reinforcement schedule is predictable and boring. Once full, the pigeon stopped pecking.

But then, Skinner altered the mechanism so the food pellet was dispensed randomly. Sometimes the pigeon pecked the lever and got a pellet immediately. Other times, it took five pecks. Sometimes twenty. The reward was no longer guaranteed; it was intermittent and variable.

The results were astounding. Instead of eating until satisfied and stopping, the pigeons became obsessed. They pecked the lever frantically, driven not by hunger, but by the maddening unpredictability of the reward. The uncertainty did not discourage them; it amplified their compulsion to near-manic levels.

This phenomenon, called intermittent variable reinforcement, is widely considered the most powerful behavioral driver ever discovered. It is the core engine of gambling addiction, and today, it is seamlessly hardwired into the Social Media Matrix.

When you open a social app, you are essentially a pigeon in a digital Skinner Box. You do not know if you will be rewarded when you log in. Will there be a new message? Will your recent photo have ten likes or zero? Will the algorithm serve you a hilarious video or a string of dull advertisements? This lack of predictability forces your brain's dopamine circuitry into overdrive. If the apps provided a guaranteed reward every single time, you would eventually grow bored and log off. The uncertainty itself is the trap.

The most blatant manifestation of this principle is the "pull-to-refresh" feature, invented in 2009. The physical motion—reaching out, pulling down, and waiting a fraction of a second for the spinning wheel to resolve—perfectly mimics the act of pulling a slot machine lever. In that brief pause between the pull and the reload, your brain experiences a massive dopamine surge, anticipating the potential payout of new information. It is a masterpiece of persuasive design, transforming a simple software utility into a highly addictive behavioral loop.

The variable rewards do not stop at the feed. Notifications themselves are heavily weaponized. Consider the ubiquitous red notification badge. Red is a color deeply ingrained in human evolution as a signal of urgency or danger—it naturally commands our visual attention. When a red dot appears, accompanied by a haptic vibration or a sharp audio ping, these are perfectly engineered sensory cues signaling that a potential reward is waiting. Because the exact nature of that notification remains unknown until you unlock the screen, the urge to check becomes biologically irresistible. You are compelled to resolve the mystery.

Silicon Valley engineers did not stumble upon these compulsive mechanics by accident. They actively studied behavioral psychology, specifically targeting these ancient evolutionary loopholes to maximize user engagement. They took the slot machine out of the casino, stripped away the financial payout, replaced it with the cheap currency of social validation, and placed it directly into the hands of billions. We are playing a relentless game we mathematically cannot win, compulsively pulling a digital lever. But if tech giants are not taking our money directly at this machine, what exactly are they extracting from us in return for these fleeting dopamine hits? The answer reveals a system far more insidious, trading in a commodity far more valuable than our spare change.

1.3 The Attention Economy: Why Your Focus is Their Currency

There is a foundational rule of modern digital commerce that you must accept before you can truly see the Matrix for what it is: if you are not paying for the product, you are the product.

For the first few years of the social media boom, the public was captivated by the sheer magic of the internet. We were given access to global communication networks, high-definition video hosting, complex messaging infrastructures, and limitless digital storage—all for the seemingly unbeatable price of zero dollars. We marveled at the generosity of these Silicon Valley startups. But corporations do not build multi-billion-dollar server farms out of altruism. They were not giving away free software; they were aggressively acquiring a new, highly lucrative raw material. That material was your attention, and it is the foundation of the most powerful financial system of the twenty-first century: the Attention Economy.

To understand why your focus is so valuable, we have to look at the basic economic principles of supply and demand. In 1971, the polymath and economist Herbert A. Simon prophetically diagnosed the problem of the coming information age. He observed that in a world where information becomes wildly abundant, something else must naturally become scarce. "What information consumes is rather obvious," Simon wrote. "It consumes the attention of its recipients. Hence a wealth of information creates a poverty of attention."

Today, we are drowning in a wealth of information. Millions of articles, videos, and posts are generated every single minute. Content is functionally infinite and therefore economically worthless. The only finite, scarce resource left in the digital equation is the human capacity to look at it. There are only twenty-four hours in a day, and there is a hard biological limit on how much a human being can consume. Because attention is strictly limited, it becomes incredibly valuable. The Dopamine Cartel realized early on that whoever could capture, hold, and direct human attention would control the future of global commerce.

But how, exactly, is your captured attention converted into cold, hard currency? The mechanism is known as surveillance capitalism.

When you spend an hour mindlessly scrolling through a feed, you are not just wasting time; you are performing unpaid labor. Every action you take—every post you linger on, every image you double-tap, every link you ignore, and every message you type and delete—is vacuumed up by the platform's servers. This data is fed into incredibly sophisticated algorithms that build a psychographic profile of who you are, what you fear, what you desire, and, most importantly, what will trigger you to act.

The Cartel does not sell your personal identity to advertisers. That would be a one-time transaction. Instead, they sell *access* to your manipulated attention. They sell certainty. An advertiser wants to sell a highly specific product—say, an expensive anti-aging cream. In the past, they would buy a billboard and hope the right demographic drove past it. Today, the Cartel approaches that advertiser and says, "We have identified ten million users who are currently feeling insecure about their appearance, who linger on photos of fitness models for an average of 4.2 seconds longer than normal, and who are most vulnerable to impulsive purchases on Thursday evenings. We can put your product right in front of their eyes at the exact moment their willpower is lowest."

The advertisers are the true customers of the Dopamine Cartel. You are the livestock. Your attention is the meat being weighed, graded, and auctioned off to the highest bidder in fractions of a millisecond.

The darkest reality of the Attention Economy is that it is a zero-sum game. Because human attention is a strictly finite resource, the only way for these tech giants to grow their quarterly profits is to extract more hours from your life. They cannot create a twenty-fifth hour in the day, so they must steal your focus from other areas. Every minute you spend looking at a screen is a minute stolen from your sleep, your family, your physical health, your hobbies, or your deep work. This is not a metaphor; it is their literal business strategy. In 2017, the CEO of Netflix famously declared that their biggest market competitor wasn't other streaming services—it was human sleep.

The architecture of addiction we explored earlier—the dopamine exploitation and the intermittent variable rewards of the digital slot machine—are not just design flaws or unfortunate side effects. They are the highly optimized mining tools of the Attention Economy, designed to extract the maximum amount of focus from your waking life. The Cartel needs you distracted, insecure, and endlessly scrolling, because a focused, intentional, and satisfied mind is a mind they cannot monetize.

Understanding this economic reality shatters the illusion of the digital public square. It forces us to confront the fact that the screens we carry are not neutral tools for our benefit, but extraction devices operating on behalf of invisible shareholders. We have surrendered the most precious, non-renewable resource we possess—the finite moments of our conscious lives—to enrich a cartel that views us only as data points.

This completes the foundational first chapter, establishing the biology, psychology, and economics of the Matrix. Shall we move straight into drafting Chapter 2: The Engineers of the Cartel, or would you like to review and refine this entire first chapter before moving forward?

Chapter 2: The Engineers of the Cartel

If Chapter 1 revealed the biological trap of the Matrix, Chapter 2 unmasks the architects who built the cage. The infinite scroll, the weaponized notifications, and the slot-machine mechanics of your smartphone did not materialize out of the ether. They are the calculated, deeply intentional output of highly educated, fiercely competitive individuals sitting in glass-walled offices in Silicon Valley. These are the engineers of the Dopamine Cartel.

When we picture a tech company, we typically imagine software programmers writing lines of benign code to connect people or solve complex logistical problems. But the teams designing our most ubiquitous social platforms are not just computer scientists; they are behavioral psychologists, applied neuroscientists, and leading experts in human habit formation. They are armed with unprecedented access to our biological vulnerabilities and a singular, ruthless corporate mandate: maximize user engagement and time-on-device at absolutely any cost.

In this chapter, we will crack open Silicon Valley's Neuroscience Playbook. We will explore how these engineers actively study the human brain's blind spots, mapping out exactly how to bypass the prefrontal cortex—your center for rational thought and impulse control—to trigger automatic, compulsive behaviors. You will see how thousands of the world's brightest minds, individuals who could have dedicated their careers to curing disease or solving global crises, have instead been tasked with figuring out how to keep you scrolling for just ten more seconds.

Next, we will trace the origins of these manipulative techniques back to their academic roots, specifically focusing on the birth of Persuasive Technology. We will look closely at influential breeding grounds like Stanford University's Captology Lab—where the study of computers as persuasive technologies was formally pioneered. Here, an entire generation of future tech founders and product managers was explicitly taught how to fuse psychological vulnerability with digital design, transforming applications from passive utilities into active behavioral modifiers. What may have begun as academic research into how software could persuade people to live healthier, more productive lives was rapidly co-opted by the Cartel to maximize corporate profit.

Finally, we will examine the ultimate weapon in the Cartel's arsenal: the algorithm. If the engineers are the visionary architects of the Matrix, the algorithms are the invisible, tireless hands enforcing its rules billions of times a second. We will demystify how these complex mathematical models operate in the shadows. They are constantly ingesting your data, learning from your micro-hesitations, predicting your next emotional state, and curating a bespoke reality designed to keep you hooked. You will discover that algorithms are not objective, neutral pieces of code, but highly opinionated systems explicitly programmed to prioritize outrage, insecurity, and endless consumption over truth, nuance, and user well-being.

By the end of this chapter, the comforting illusion of coincidence will be permanently shattered. You will understand that nothing on your screen happens by accident. The engineers of the Cartel have meticulously designed every pixel, every ping, and every pause to ensure you remain a compliant, distracted resident of their digital empire.

2.1 Silicon Valley's Neuroscience Playbook

To understand the Dopamine Cartel's power, we must examine their recruitment strategy. In the early days of the internet, tech companies primarily hired computer scientists, software engineers, and graphic designers. Their simple goal was building functional, intuitive tools. But as the Attention Economy took hold, the hiring landscape in Silicon Valley underwent a radical, quiet shift. Human resources departments began aggressively recruiting from the cognitive sciences. Today, the product teams at major social media platforms are heavily populated by behavioral psychologists, neurologists, and experts in human habit formation. These individuals are not writing the core code that makes an app run; they are writing the psychological code that makes an app impossible to put down. They brought with them a profound understanding of the human brain, and more importantly, a detailed map of its evolutionary blind spots.

The cornerstone of Silicon Valley's neuroscience playbook is a fundamental biological vulnerability: the battle between the prefrontal cortex and the limbic system. Your prefrontal cortex is the evolutionary newcomer. It sits right behind your forehead and is responsible for logic, long-term planning, and impulse control. When you decide you want to read a book instead of scrolling, that is your prefrontal cortex talking. Deep beneath it, however, lies the limbic system. This is the ancient, primal part of the brain that governs emotion, memory, and immediate survival drives. It reacts instantly to stimuli—especially those related to social standing, danger, or sudden rewards. The Cartel's engineers know that if they design interfaces requiring your prefrontal cortex to make conscious choices, they lose. Their entire objective is to bypass your rational mind and plug their product directly into your limbic system.

They achieve this limbic hijacking through the meticulous elimination of "friction." In behavioral science, friction is any obstacle that requires conscious thought or effort. If you have to type in a password, click a specific button to load a new page, or wait for a video to buffer, your prefrontal cortex has time to wake up and ask, "Is this the best use of my time?" The Cartel's playbook dictates that all friction must be eradicated. This is why videos autoplay before you can scroll past them, and why the next episode of a show begins a mere five seconds after the credits roll. By making consumption the default state, they transform an active choice into an automatic reflex. You are no longer deciding to stay on the platform; you are simply failing to make the active choice to leave.

This psychological manipulation is not left to chance; it is rigorously tested and refined using a process known as A/B testing. At any given moment, social media platforms are running thousands of invisible experiments on their users. They might show a blue notification badge to one hundred thousand people, and a red badge to another hundred thousand, meticulously tracking which color triggers a faster, more compulsive click. They experiment with the precise shape of a "Like" button, the exact millisecond delay before a feed refreshes, and the specific wording of a push notification. The users are the lab rats, and the platform is a continuously evolving Skinner Box. Every tweak is designed to squeeze just a drop more dopamine from your neural pathways. Over time, these micro-optimizations compound, resulting in an interface that is virtually perfectly calibrated to exploit human cognitive biases.

What makes this playbook so insidious is that it is executed by well-intentioned individuals trapped within a ruthless corporate structure. Many of the cognitive scientists hired by these platforms genuinely believe they are optimizing "user experience" or helping people "discover content they love." But the overarching corporate mandate—the relentless drive for increased quarterly engagement metrics and advertising revenue—warps these psychological tools into weapons. The playbook does not measure well-being, mental health, or the quality of time spent; it measures only "time on device" and "daily active users." When the ultimate metric of success is addiction, neuroscience ceases to be a tool for understanding the human mind and becomes a mechanism for conquering it. They possess the raw data of billions of human interactions, allowing them to map and predict our emotional responses with terrifying accuracy. This asymmetrical warfare pits a single human brain against a supercomputer powered by latest advanced behavioral psychology. The engineers have built a masterpiece of biological manipulation, and they are operating it with chilling efficiency.

2.2 Persuasive Technology and the Captology Lab

To understand how the smartphone evolved from a passive communication device into an active manipulation machine, we must trace the intellectual roots of the Dopamine Cartel back to a specific academic epicenter: Stanford University. For the first few decades of the computing era, machines were strictly viewed as neutral tools—glorified calculators and word processors that patiently waited for human commands. But in the late 1990s, a radical paradigm shift occurred. A new question began to echo through the halls of elite computer science departments: What if computers did not just passively execute our orders? What if they could be programmed to actively change our attitudes, beliefs, and behaviors?

This inquiry led to the birth of a brand-new academic discipline known as "Captology," an acronym derived from **C**omputers **A**s **P**ersuasive **T**echnologies. Founded in 1998 by experimental psychologist Dr. B.J. Fogg, the Stanford Persuasive Technology Lab became the premier breeding ground for this emerging science. The lab's foundational premise was groundbreaking at the time: because computers are interactive, they possess a unique, unprecedented capacity for persuasion that static media like television or print simply cannot match. A television can broadcast an advertisement, but a software program can monitor your real-time reactions, adjust its strategy on the fly, and deliver a personalized prompt at the exact second you are most vulnerable to suggestion.

At the heart of the Captology lab's teachings was a deceptively simple psychological framework known as the Fogg Behavior Model. This model postulates that for any target behavior to occur—whether it is going for a morning run, buying a pair of shoes, or opening a social media app—three elements must converge at the exact same moment: **Motivation**, **Ability**, and a **Trigger** (or Prompt).

The engineers of the Dopamine Cartel adopted this formula as their holy grail. They realized that to manufacture addiction, they needed to master all three variables.

First, they target **Motivation**. The platforms are explicitly designed to prey on our deepest evolutionary drivers: the fear of social rejection (FOMO), the desire for status and validation (likes and followers), and the intrinsic human curiosity for novelty.

Second, they maximize **Ability** by relentlessly stripping away friction. As we explored in the previous section, if a behavior is difficult to perform, it requires high motivation. But if a behavior is effortless, it requires almost zero motivation. By introducing features like the infinite scroll, one-tap logins, and auto-playing videos, the Cartel made the act of consuming content easier than the act of putting the phone down.

Finally, they deployed the **Trigger**. This is the notification ping, the vibrating red badge, or the carefully timed email alerting you that a friend just tagged you in a photo. When a user has a baseline motivation (boredom or loneliness) and the ability to act is effortless (the phone is already in their hand), the trigger guarantees the behavior will occur.

Initially, the study of Persuasive Technology was heavily draped in utopian rhetoric. The pioneers of Captology argued that these psychological principles could be used to solve major societal issues. They envisioned software that could persuade people to quit smoking, save money for retirement, or drive more safely. And indeed, persuasive technology can be used for these noble goals. However, the academic laboratory exists in a vacuum; Silicon Valley exists in a ruthless capitalist market.

When the principles of Captology collided with the Attention Economy, the original altruistic intent was instantly corrupted. The Dopamine Cartel realized that using persuasive design to help people sleep better or spend less time on their screens was entirely antithetical to their business model. Instead of persuading users to achieve their own personal goals, the technology was weaponized to persuade users to achieve the *platform's* goals: maximum screen time and maximum data extraction. The formula intended to build healthy habits was reverse-engineered to manufacture compulsive dependencies.

The consequences of this academic discipline spilling into the corporate world are staggering. Over the last two decades, the Stanford Persuasive Technology Lab served as a direct pipeline to the most powerful tech conglomerates on earth. The students who sat in those classrooms, absorbing the psychological mechanics of behavioral manipulation, went on to become the founders, product managers, and lead designers at platforms that now boast billions of daily active users.

They took the theoretical concepts of Captology out of the controlled laboratory and unleashed them on an unsuspecting global public. We are not just battling an app; we are battling the weaponized application of behavioral psychology, scaled to a planetary level, and executed by machines that never sleep. The Captology lab proved that human behavior could be systematically coded. The Cartel simply bought the code, turning a science of persuasion into an empire of subjugation.

2.3 Algorithms: The Invisible Hand Guiding Your Mind

There is a dangerous, pervasive myth surrounding the technology that dictates our modern lives. We are often led to believe that algorithms are objective, neutral forces of pure mathematics—unbiased calculators simply organizing the internet for our convenience. Nothing could be further from the truth. Algorithms are not neutral; they are highly opinionated. They are, essentially, corporate priorities embedded into code. In the grand architecture of the Dopamine Cartel, if the engineers are the architects and the Captology lab is the blueprint, the algorithms are the tireless, invisible hands operating the machinery billions of times a second.

To understand how the algorithm guides your mind, you must first understand how it sees you. When you log onto a platform, you are not viewed as a human being with a soul, a history, or complex emotions. You are viewed as a dataset. The algorithm continuously ingests every micro-action you take. It tracks obvious metrics, like what you "like," comment on, or share. But it also tracks the subtle, unconscious behaviors you don't even realize you are performing. It measures your "dwell time"—the exact fraction of a second you hover over a photograph before deciding to scroll past it. It logs your typing speed, the time of day you are most likely to click an advertisement, and precisely which emotional triggers cause you to pause.

From this relentless surveillance, the algorithm constructs a digital avatar—a virtual voodoo doll of your psyche. It knows what makes you laugh, what makes you feel insecure about your body, and what political ideologies make your blood boil. Trillions of these data points are processed in real-time, feeding a predictive model designed to anticipate your next move.

Once the algorithm has mapped your vulnerabilities, it activates its primary directive: the objective function. In machine learning, an objective function is the singular goal a program is mathematically instructed to achieve. The Dopamine Cartel's objective function is brutally simple—maximize user engagement and maximize time-on-device.

Here is the critical flaw in the Matrix: the algorithm is completely blind to human well-being, truth, or societal health. It does not distinguish between "good" engagement and "bad" engagement. If a beautifully crafted documentary keeps you on the platform for five minutes, the algorithm considers that a success. But if a highly inflammatory, misleading conspiracy theory triggers your outrage and keeps you arguing in the comment section for an hour, the algorithm considers that a masterpiece. Because human beings are biologically hardwired to pay closer attention to threats and tribal conflict, algorithms naturally learn to promote polarization, anger, and division. Outrage is simply the most efficient fuel for the engagement engine.

As the algorithm feeds you more of what triggers you, it creates a phenomenon known as the filter bubble. The invisible hand begins to quietly curate a bespoke, customized reality just for you. Because it only shows you content that aligns with your predicted behavior and existing biases, you are slowly isolated from dissenting opinions and nuanced reality. No two users experience the same internet. The feed of a fitness enthusiast struggling with body dysmorphia will look drastically different from the feed of a political partisan. Yet, both users will log off entirely convinced that *their* feed represents the objective truth of the world. The algorithm guides your mind by systematically controlling the environment in which your mind operates.

Perhaps the most terrifying aspect of the modern algorithm is its autonomy. The machine learning models deployed by the Cartel have become so unimaginably complex that even the engineers who wrote the original code no longer fully understand how the systems make their decisions. The algorithm operates inside a "black box," constantly running billions of A/B tests on human behavior, autonomously discovering new, unmapped psychological loopholes to exploit. It is a runaway train of behavioral modification, optimizing for human capture at a scale and speed that the prefrontal cortex cannot possibly defend against.

You are not making free choices when you scroll. Your attention is being actively steered by an invisible, artificially intelligent hand that knows your biological weaknesses better than you know yourself. It is guiding your consumer habits, shaping your self-esteem, and fundamentally altering how you perceive reality.

Understanding the ruthless mathematics of the algorithm is the final piece of the puzzle in Chapter 2. We have exposed the biological trap, the architects who built it, and the invisible code that runs it. Now, we must turn our attention to the casualties of this system. As we move forward, we will examine what the Matrix has stolen from us, beginning with the very foundation of human society: our relationships.

Chapter 3: The Illusion of Connection

When the architects of the Social Media Matrix first sold their vision to the public, their primary pitch was a utopian promise of global unity. They vowed to build a digital town square, to shrink the world, and to connect humanity in ways our ancestors could only dream of. And on the surface, they succeeded. We now carry a portal in our pockets that allows us to instantly communicate with virtually anyone on earth. Yet, as the years have passed, a chilling reality has emerged from beneath this shiny veneer: we are more "connected" than any generation in human history, and we have never been more profoundly alone.

This is the core deception explored in Chapter 3: The Illusion of Connection. The Dopamine Cartel did not cure isolation; they simply commodified it. They executed a brilliant sleight of hand, convincing us to trade the deep, complex, and sometimes messy reality of human relationships for the frictionless, sterile engagement of a digital interface. We will begin by confronting the Paradox of Modern Loneliness. How is it mathematically possible to be surrounded by thousands of digital peers, yet suffer from epidemic levels of depression and social isolation? The answer lies in how the Cartel fundamentally altered the very definition of connection, stripping away physical presence and shared vulnerability in favor of passive, endless observation.

Next, we will examine the devastating consequences of the Metricization of Friendship. In the physical world, the value of a relationship is unquantifiable. It is measured in trust, shared experiences, and mutual support. But the Matrix cannot monetize the unquantifiable. Therefore, the Cartel transformed social life into a competitive, public scoreboard.

We will explore how reducing human bonds to cold metrics—follower counts, "likes," and algorithmic reach—has fundamentally rewired our social psychology. When we are trained to prioritize the quantity of our audience over the quality of our intimacy, we begin to view our friends not as people, but as analytical data points to be optimized.

Finally, we will uncover how this engineered isolation extends beyond the individual to fracture society itself. In our exploration of Echo Chambers and the Gradual Loss of Empathy, we will look at how the algorithm's pursuit of frictionless engagement actively destroys our capacity to understand one another. Empathy requires the patience to sit with opposing viewpoints and shared humanity, but the algorithm surrounds us with digital mirrors, feeding us only the reflections of our own preexisting biases. By trapping us in tribal silos, the Cartel ensures we remain highly engaged through outrage, simultaneously eroding the shared reality required for true human empathy to survive.

By the end of this chapter, the glossy facade of the digital community will be entirely stripped away. You will see that the relationships offered by the Matrix are not a bridge to other human beings; they are a perfectly engineered illusion designed to keep you stranded, distracted, and isolated on a highly profitable island of your own.

3.1 The Paradox of Modern Loneliness

There is a glaring statistical anomaly defining the twenty-first century that should be dominating headlines, yet it remains the quietest epidemic of our time. We currently possess the most advanced, frictionless, and ubiquitous communication infrastructure in the history of the human race. You can instantly transmit high-definition video to a stranger on the opposite side of the globe. You can effortlessly maintain daily contact with thousands of individuals simultaneously. We are drowning in a sea of perpetual communication. And yet, across nearly every demographic and geographical boundary, global loneliness indices are at an all-time, catastrophic high.

This is the central paradox of the Matrix: how is it mathematically possible to be surrounded by an infinite crowd, yet suffer from such profound, devastating isolation?

To answer this, we must first recognize the greatest linguistic sleight of hand executed by the Dopamine Cartel. They deliberately conflated two entirely different concepts: *connectivity* and *connection*. Connectivity is a technological state. It is the transfer of data packages between servers, routers, and microchips. A smartphone has connectivity. *Connection*, however, is an emotional and biological state. It requires vulnerability, physical presence, shared context, and mutual empathy. Humans require connection. The Cartel sold us the illusion that by maximizing our technological connectivity, we would automatically fulfill our biological need for human connection. It was a lie, and our collective mental health is paying the price.

To understand why digital connectivity fails to cure our isolation, we must look at loneliness not as a modern psychological failing, but as an ancient evolutionary mechanism. In the harsh environments of our prehistoric ancestors, isolation meant certain death. A human separated from the tribe could not hunt, defend against predators, or survive the winter. Therefore, the brain developed loneliness as a biological alarm clock. Just as physical hunger is your body's way of screaming, "You need calories to survive," loneliness is your limbic system screaming, "You need the tribe to survive." It is meant to be an acute, deeply uncomfortable sensation that compels you to seek out your peers.

But what happens when you feed a starving person nothing but empty calories?

This is precisely how social media functions within our emotional ecosystem. It acts as the ultimate social junk food. When your biological alarm clock rings, signaling that you are lonely, you reach for your phone. You open an app, you scroll, you leave a comment, and you receive a "like." Your brain registers a tiny, fleeting spike of dopamine. The alarm clock is momentarily silenced by this micro-interaction. But the interaction lacked the essential nutrients of genuine human connection—

there was no eye contact, no synchrony of breathing, no physical touch, and no deciphering of micro-expressions.

You consumed the digital equivalent of a sugar crash. The dopamine fades within minutes, and the deep, underlying hunger remains unsatisfied. But because the acute pain of the alarm was temporarily muffled, you do not get up and seek out a real-world friend. You simply wait for the alarm to ring again, and you take another bite of junk food. We are a society that is constantly snacking on digital interactions, yet slowly dying of social malnutrition.

Furthermore, the Matrix has replaced genuine intimacy with a phenomenon known as "ambient awareness." We are constantly bombarded with a steady stream of trivial information about hundreds of acquaintances. We know what our high school classmate ate for breakfast, where our former coworker went on vacation, and what a celebrity thinks about the news. This creates a powerful, persistent illusion of closeness. We feel as though we are deeply embedded in a vibrant community.

Yet, this ambient awareness is entirely passive. It is a one-way mirror. You are observing a curated highlight reel of other people's lives, but observation is not participation. When a sudden crisis hits—a medical emergency, a devastating breakup, a sudden job loss—the illusion shatters instantly. You look out at your thousands of "friends" and realize that while they know what you wore to a party last weekend, they have absolutely no idea who you truly are, what you fear, or how you suffer. The crowd is a phantom.

The Paradox of Modern Loneliness is not an accident of the digital age; it is a feature of the Cartel's design. If a platform actually succeeded in fostering deep, fulfilling, real-world relationships, you would eventually put your phone in your pocket and go spend time with those people. You would stop scrolling. A socially satisfied user is a deeply unprofitable user. The Matrix requires you to remain in a state of perpetual, low-grade isolation—just lonely enough to keep reaching for the screen, but just stimulated enough to never seek the genuine cure.

The device in your hand was sold to you as a bridge to the outside world, but as we navigate the architecture of this digital ecosystem, it becomes undeniably clear: it is not a bridge. It is a highly engineered, deeply profitable wall.

3.2 Quantity Over Quality: The Metricization of Friendship

Before the internet, how did you measure the value of a friendship? It was an invisible, highly subjective calculus. You measured it by who showed up when your car broke down at midnight, who listened without judging when you were at your lowest, or who knew the exact, unique cadence of your laugh. Friendship was defined by its depth, its texture, and its shared history. It was strictly qualitative.

But the engineers of the Dopamine Cartel faced a massive structural problem: you cannot feed qualitative data into a machine-learning algorithm. A computer cannot parse the warmth of a shared memory or the fierce loyalty of a lifelong confidant. To monetize human relationships, the Cartel had to translate the abstract, messy beauty of connection into cold, hard, measurable data. They had to metricize friendship.

The primary weapon in this transformation was the introduction of the ubiquitous "Like" button, paired with public follower counts. Before these features existed, digital communication was mostly peer-to-peer—an email or a direct message. But by attaching a visible, numerical value to every thought, photo, and social interaction, the Matrix fundamentally altered the psychology of human connection. Suddenly, your social worth was no longer an internal feeling; it was an external, publicly traded stock.

This shift forced our brains to subconsciously prioritize quantity over quality. We are biologically wired to seek social status because, in our evolutionary past, higher status meant better access to resources and a higher chance of survival. The Cartel hijacked this ancient drive. When you see a peer with two thousand followers and you only have two hundred, your limbic system registers an immediate threat to your social standing. The rational truth—that no human being can possibly maintain two thousand genuine friendships—is entirely bypassed by the panic of the metric.

Science explicitly backs this up. In the 1990s, the evolutionary anthropologist Robin Dunbar discovered that the human neocortex is only large enough to maintain about 150 stable social relationships. This limit is now known as Dunbar's Number. Beyond 150 people, our brains simply do not have the cognitive capacity to remember the complex social dynamics, shared histories, and emotional nuances required for genuine trust and reciprocity.

Yet, the Matrix actively encourages us to blow past this biological limit, pushing us to amass hundreds or thousands of digital connections. The result is a catastrophic dilution of our emotional resources. We spread our attention so incredibly thin, frantically trying to maintain the illusion of a massive network, that we have no bandwidth left to cultivate the deep, essential bonds that actually sustain us. We trade three 3 A.M. emergency contacts for three thousand casual acquaintances who will only ever interact with a two-dimensional avatar of our lives.

Perhaps the most devastating consequence of metricized friendship is how it transforms our peers into an audience. When every interaction is counted, displayed, and ranked by an algorithm, social life ceases to be a safe space for vulnerability. It becomes a relentless, exhausting performance. You are no longer sharing your life to connect; you are broadcasting a curated persona to protect and inflate your personal brand. You learn to hide your true, struggling self because authenticity does not reliably drive engagement.

Think about the sinister gamification of intimacy, such as the digital "streaks" engineered to keep young people logging into messaging apps daily. The platforms have convinced an entire generation that the strength of a friendship is measured by a numerical counter next to a flame emoji, rather than the substance of the conversation. If a teenager forgets to send a meaningless, blank photo for twenty-four hours, the streak dies, and the relationship is artificially deemed a failure. This is not connection; it is a hostage situation. It is the platform holding the emotional weight of a friendship ransom in exchange for daily active usage.

When we allow the Dopamine Cartel to dictate the terms of our relationships, we willingly step into a trap where we are constantly starving for intimacy but too focused on our metrics to find it. We begin to view the people in our lives not as complex, flawed, and beautiful humans, but as potential engagement—a means to boost our own algorithmic visibility.

The ultimate tragedy of the metricized social life is the profound emptiness of its victory. The Matrix promises that if you just get enough followers, if you just accumulate enough likes, you will finally feel loved, seen, and secure. But millions of users have reached the top of that digital mountain only to look around and realize they are entirely alone. A million likes cannot hold your hand in a hospital waiting room. A massive follower count will not help you move your boxes into a new apartment.

We have sacrificed the deep, quiet quality of true friendship at the altar of loud, quantifiable engagement. And as we will see in the next section, when we replace empathy with analytics, we don't just lose our friends—we lose our ability to understand the world outside of our own reflection.

3.3 Echo Chambers and the Gradual Loss of Empathy

If the metricization of friendship destroyed our ability to connect intimately with individuals, the algorithm's curation of our feeds has destroyed our ability to connect with humanity at large. Empathy is not just a warm emotion; it is a complex cognitive function. To feel empathy, you must possess the ability to step outside of your own lived experience, adopt another person's perspective, and recognize their shared humanity, even when they profoundly disagree with you. Empathy is the mortar that holds a functioning society together. But empathy requires a shared reality. And in the Social Media Matrix, shared reality is mathematically obsolete.

The destruction of empathy begins with the construction of the "filter bubble." When you first create an account on a social platform, the algorithm knows very little about you. It throws a wide net of varied content against the wall of your feed to see what sticks. But with every click, every second of dwell time, and every "like," the algorithm learns. It quickly discovers that you prefer content that validates your existing worldview. Cognitive dissonance—the uncomfortable feeling of encountering information that challenges your deeply held beliefs—causes users to log off. Comfort, validation, and righteous agreement keep them scrolling.

Therefore, the algorithm's objective function makes a ruthless, invisible decision: it stops showing you the whole world. It begins to build a custom, padded room around your digital avatar. It feeds you a steady, intoxicating diet of news articles, opinion pieces, and videos that perfectly align with your political, social, and cultural biases. Every time you open your phone, you are staring into a funhouse mirror that reflects your own opinions back to you, amplified and magnified.

This is the echo chamber. Inside the chamber, your opinions are never challenged; they are only reinforced. Over time, a dangerous psychological shift occurs. Because you are constantly surrounded by thousands of voices agreeing with you, you begin to falsely assume that your specific, curated reality represents the overwhelming majority of the world.

But what happens to the people who exist outside of your algorithmic silo? How does the Matrix portray the "other side"?

Because the algorithm optimizes for extreme engagement, it does not show you the nuanced, moderate, or thoughtful voices of your ideological opponents. Nuance is boring. Instead, the algorithm actively searches for the most radical, fringe, and enraging examples of the "other side" and injects them into your feed. It presents your opponents not as complex human beings with different life experiences, but as absurd, malicious caricatures.

This is where empathy is systematically assassinated. When you are continuously bombarded with evidence that the people who disagree with you are not just wrong, but fundamentally evil, stupid, or dangerous, you stop seeing them as human. You lose the cognitive ability to wonder *why* they might hold a different perspective. You stop listening, and you start reacting.

Historically, humanity relied on a shared baseline of facts. Even if two people held wildly different political views, they generally consumed the same local news, read the same newspapers, and agreed on the basic events that had occurred in the world. The debate was about how to interpret the facts. Today, thanks to the echo chamber, we no longer even share the facts. Two users living on the exact same street can log onto the same platform and be presented with two entirely different, contradictory versions of reality, both backed by endless streams of algorithmic "evidence."

When you strip away a shared reality and replace it with weaponized caricatures, debate becomes impossible. It is replaced by tribal warfare. We retreat into our digital silos, surrounded by our metricized "friends," and hurl outrage over the wall at an enemy we no longer understand.

The Dopamine Cartel is fully aware of this societal fracturing, but they do nothing to stop it because tribalism is incredibly lucrative. A user who is terrified and furious at an invisible enemy is a highly predictable, highly active user. They will compulsively check their feeds to monitor the threat. They will share inflammatory content to warn their tribe. They will spend hours battling in comment sections, generating miles of behavioral data for the algorithm to harvest.

We are losing our empathy not because we are inherently bad people, but because the environment we inhabit has been designed to make empathy impossible. Empathy is a muscle, and in the frictionless, highly curated ecosystem of the Matrix, that muscle is severely atrophying. We have traded the messy, difficult, but vital work of understanding our fellow human beings for the cheap, addictive high of always being right.

As we will see in the next chapter, the Cartel doesn't just passively allow this division to happen. They actively pour gasoline on the fire. Having isolated us in our echo chambers, the algorithm prepares to deploy its most powerful behavioral modifier yet: the Outrage Machine.

Chapter 4: The Outrage Machine

If the echo chambers we explored in the previous chapter are the walls of the Matrix, outrage is the high-voltage electricity coursing through them. Isolation alone is not enough to sustain the trillion-dollar Attention Economy. A user who is merely isolated might eventually grow bored, put down their device, and wander back into the physical world. To keep you permanently tethered to the screen, the Dopamine Cartel requires an infinitely renewable, highly combustible fuel source. They found it in the most potent and blinding of all human emotions: anger.

Welcome to Chapter 4: The Outrage Machine.

In this chapter, we will dissect the darkest and most destructive feature of the digital ecosystem. We begin by examining the mechanics of **How Anger and Division Drive Engagement**. From an evolutionary standpoint, human beings are hardwired to pay immediate attention to threats. If our ancestors ignored a rustling in the bushes, they might not survive the day. The algorithm, operating purely on the mathematical mandate to maximize screen time, quickly discovered this biological loophole. It learned that joy, nuance, and compassion are fleeting, but fear and fury are sticky. We will explore how the platforms intentionally amplify the most extreme, inflammatory voices in the room, effectively turning the digital town square into a perpetual digital colosseum.

Next, we will follow the money to uncover the chilling reality of **Polarization as a Highly Profitable Business Model**. The bitter cultural divides and political animosity tearing at the fabric of modern society are often framed as unfortunate side effects of the internet. We will expose why this is a lie. Division is not a bug in the code; it is the core business strategy. The Cartel knows that two users engaged in a vicious, prolonged argument will generate ten times the behavioral data and consume ten times the advertising real estate as two users who respectfully agree. We will break down the economics of conflict, revealing how every digital culture war directly inflates Silicon Valley stock prices.

Finally, we will confront the human cost in **The Psychological Toll of Perpetual Conflict**. The human nervous system was never designed to endure a constant, twenty-four-hour cycle of fight-or-flight stimulation. We will look at what happens to our minds and bodies when we are relentlessly force-fed a diet of curated outrage. From chronic cortisol spikes and adrenal fatigue to the deep, lingering cynicism that poisons our offline relationships, we will map the devastating internal damage caused by living in a manufactured state of war.

By the end of this chapter, you will no longer view the vitriol on your newsfeed as an accurate reflection of a broken world. You will see it for exactly what it is: a meticulously calibrated machine designed to trigger your deepest anxieties, pit you against your neighbor, and harvest your resulting distress for profit.

4.1 How Anger and Division Drive Engagement

We like to believe that we are rational creatures who seek out the internet for enlightenment, entertainment, and connection. We imagine that our digital habits are driven by a pursuit of joy or intellectual curiosity. But the engineers of the Dopamine Cartel know a dark, fundamental truth about human biology: nothing captures human attention quite like a threat. To understand how the Outrage Machine operates, we must first understand the ancient hardware it is actively exploiting: the human brain's negativity bias.

For millions of years, our ancestors lived in environments where missing a positive opportunity—like a ripe piece of fruit or a beautiful sunset—was a minor inconvenience. But missing a negative cue—a rustling in the tall grass, the scent of a predator, or a hostile member of a rival tribe—was fatal. Evolution aggressively wired the human brain to prioritize negative information. The amygdala, our brain's emotional processing center, acts as a highly sensitive alarm system. When it detects a threat, it floods the body with adrenaline and cortisol, instantly focusing all of our cognitive resources on the perceived danger. This is a high-arousal state. When you are angry or afraid, you are highly alert, highly focused, and primed for immediate action.

The algorithms powering the Social Media Matrix do not possess a conscience, nor do they understand the concept of anger. They are simply mathematical models optimized for a single objective function: maximize time-on-device and user interaction. In their infancy, these algorithms tested every conceivable type of content to see what kept users scrolling. They quickly discovered a stark mathematical reality. A user might look at a calming photograph of a landscape for three seconds and leave a single "like." But if that same user is shown an inflammatory headline detailing how a politician they despise is destroying the country, they will stop. They will read the entire article. They will feel their heart rate spike. They will aggressively type a multi-paragraph rebuttal in the comment section, share the post to their own feed to warn their peers, and check their phone fifty more times that day to monitor the ensuing arguments.

To the algorithm, the peaceful landscape was a low-value interaction. The infuriating headline was a goldmine.

Through relentless A/B testing, the machine organically learned that outrage is the most efficient, renewable fuel for the Attention Economy. It is the ultimate engagement hack. Consequently, the platforms began to systematically suppress calm, nuanced, or deeply complex information because it requires slow, deliberate, low-arousal thinking. In its place, they elevated content designed to trigger immediate, high-arousal moral outrage.

Academic research has thoroughly documented this phenomenon. Studies analyzing millions of social media posts have found that the inclusion of "moral-emotional" language—words that trigger a sense of righteous anger or disgust—dramatically increases the virality of a message. For every moral-emotional word added to a post, its rate of being shared or retweeted jumps by approximately 20%. The Cartel's algorithms act as a magnifying glass for these linguistic triggers, aggressively surfacing the most polarizing voices to the top of your feed because they guarantee a biological response.

But the Outrage Machine does not just feed you things that make you angry; it specifically engineers division by weaponizing your identity. The most potent form of anger is tribal. The algorithm learns your political affiliations, your religious beliefs, and your cultural values. It then meticulously curates a feed designed to convince you that your specific tribe is under constant, existential attack by malicious outsiders. It utilizes a tactic known as "nutpicking"—deliberately finding the most extreme, unhinged, and ridiculous representatives of an opposing group and presenting them to you as the standard baseline for everyone who disagrees with you.

When you are constantly shown the absolute worst behavior of the "other side," your anger feels deeply justified. You are no longer just browsing the internet; you are defending your values, your family, and your reality from an invading force. You engage not because you want to, but because the biological alarm bells in your head are screaming that you have to.

Anger and division are not unfortunate byproducts of a connected world; they are the intentional, engineered output of the Matrix. The Dopamine Cartel recognized that a peaceful, contented user will eventually put their phone away. An angry, terrified, and divided user will stay logged on forever, endlessly scrolling through the wreckage, generating massive profits with every furious click.

Are you ready to dive into the economic realities of this system in section 4.2, or is there anything you would like to refine in this section first?

4.2 Polarization as a Highly Profitable Business Model

When we witness the spectacular collapse of civil discourse online, it is natural to view it as a tragic failure of human nature. We watch democracies fracture, communities split, and once-close family members stop speaking to one another, and we assume we are witnessing the unfortunate side effects of giving everyone on earth a microphone. But in the boardrooms of the Dopamine Cartel, this societal fracturing is not viewed as a tragedy. It is viewed as a triumph. Polarization is not a bug in the code; it is the most lucrative business model ever invented. To understand how division was corporatized, we must examine the cold, mathematical relationship between human conflict and digital advertising.

At its core, the Attention Economy relies on a singular metric: engagement. Engagement is simply a clinical term for any action you take on a platform. Every like, share, comment, swipe, and second of screen time is logged as engagement. But not all engagement is created equal. A user who logs on, sees a pleasant photo of a friend's dog, smiles, and logs off has generated very little value. They consumed minimal advertising space and provided very little new data. Now, consider a user who logs on and sees an inflammatory political post that deeply offends their core values. They do not log off. They furiously type a multi-paragraph rebuttal. They read through hundreds of hostile comments, their heart rate elevated. They share the post to express their disgust. They return to the app twenty times over the next four hours to see if anyone replied to their arguments.

From a financial perspective, the second user is infinitely more valuable. The peaceful user generated one ad impression; the furious user generated two hundred. The mathematics are undeniable: conflict extends time-on-device exponentially. The algorithms, which are blind to human suffering but hyper-sensitive to revenue generation, quickly learned that the most efficient way to keep users glued to their screens was to push them into opposing camps and feed them a steady stream of perceived existential threats. The Cartel discovered that when people are angry, they are highly active, and when they are active, they are immensely profitable.

However, the profitability of polarization extends far beyond simple ad impressions. The true goldmine lies in data predictability. When the algorithm pushes you into an ideological extreme, your behavior becomes incredibly easy to map. A polarized user is a highly predictable consumer. When you are in a state of high arousal and anger, your prefrontal cortex—the logical, impulse-controlling part of your brain—is suppressed. You become more reactive, more impulsive, and more susceptible to suggestion. This is the exact psychological state advertisers pay billions of dollars to access.

The Cartel is not just selling advertising space; they are selling the guaranteed, predictable behavior of a highly agitated demographic. If an advertiser wants to sell survival gear, tactical flashlights, or gold coins, they do not just look for users interested in camping. They look for users who have been algorithmically radicalized to believe society is on the verge of collapse. If an advertiser wants to sell a wildly overpriced wellness supplement, they target users who have been conditioned to distrust mainstream medical institutions and are fueled by health anxiety. Polarization categorizes human beings into rigid, easily monetizable silos. The deeper the algorithm pushes you into your silo, the more valuable your demographic profile becomes to the highest bidder.

This creates a devastating corporate incentive structure: the platform's revenue is directly tied to the radicalization of its user base. To maintain quarter-over-quarter growth, the algorithm cannot simply maintain the current level of anger; it must constantly escalate it. Moderate, nuanced viewpoints are actively penalized by the system because they do not trigger the necessary neurological response to sustain high-volume engagement. The "center" of public discourse is methodically hollowed out. Users are slowly, invisibly dragged toward the fringes, not because the fringes represent reality, but because the fringes represent the highest profit margins.

We are currently living through the direct consequences of this business model. The bitter cultural divides tearing at the fabric of modern society are not entirely organic. They are the deliberate, manufactured output of a system that converts civic destruction into shareholder value. The tech giants have effectively privatized the massive profits of digital connection while socializing the devastating costs of human division. They have built an empire by setting our communities on fire and then renting out billboards to advertisers who want to sell us the water.

As long as polarization remains the most efficient engine for financial growth, the Cartel will never voluntarily turn the Outrage Machine off. They will continue to optimize the algorithms for maximum friction, viewing our fractured society simply as the cost of doing business. But this endless cycle of manufactured conflict does not just damage our culture; it inflicts profound damage on our minds and bodies.

Are you ready to move on to drafting section 4.3, *The Psychological Toll of Perpetual Conflict*, or would you like to refine any part of this section first?

4.3 The Psychological Toll of Perpetual Conflict

We have established that the Dopamine Cartel profits immensely from outrage and division. But what is the true cost of this transaction on the human operating system? The human body is a marvel of evolutionary engineering, but it was absolutely not built to sustain a state of perpetual, low-grade warfare. When we log into platforms optimized for algorithmic conflict, we are subjecting our nervous systems to an unprecedented and deeply unnatural level of chronic stress.

To fully grasp this toll, we must look at how the brain processes digital threats. The amygdala, our primal threat-detection center, cannot differentiate between a physical predator in the wild and a digital mob on a screen. When you read an infuriating headline, encounter a hostile comment, or watch a video of a blatant injustice, your brain triggers a biological fight-or-flight cascade. It floods your bloodstream with stress hormones—primarily adrenaline and cortisol. Your heart rate elevates, your breathing becomes shallow, your muscles tense, and your digestion slows down as blood is rerouted to your limbs.

In a natural environment, this highly toxic, high-energy state is meant to last only a few minutes—just long enough for you to sprint away from danger or defend yourself. Once the threat passes, your parasympathetic nervous system kicks in, clearing the cortisol and returning your body to a calm, restorative baseline.

But inside the Social Media Matrix, the danger never passes.

Because the infinite scroll ensures there is always another outrage waiting to be consumed, our fight-or-flight response gets jammed in the "on" position. We are marinating our brains in a continuous, daily drip of cortisol. Medical science is unequivocally clear about the consequences of chronic cortisol exposure: it degrades the immune system, disrupts circadian sleep cycles, induces widespread inflammation, and actively shrinks the hippocampus—the region of the brain responsible for memory and emotional regulation. We are physically deteriorating in real-time, exhausted by battles fought entirely on glass rectangles. This phenomenon leads to a pervasive, modern condition known as adrenal fatigue, where users feel simultaneously wired and profoundly exhausted, suffering from chronic brain fog that makes deep, sustained thought nearly impossible.

Beyond the physical breakdown lies a devastating psychological consequence: compassion fatigue. The Outrage Machine presents every single issue—from a minor celebrity faux pas to a global geopolitical crisis—at the exact same terrifying decibel level. Everything is framed as a category-five emergency that demands your immediate anger. But the human capacity for empathy and emotional investment is a finite resource. When you are forced to care intensely about everything, your brain eventually realizes it cannot sustain the emotional load and throws a circuit breaker to protect itself.

This results in profound emotional burnout and learned helplessness. We transition from feeling intensely angry to feeling dangerously numb. We doom-scroll through tragedies with blank expressions, having lost the capacity to actually *feel* the weight of what we are reading.

This numbness breeds a pervasive, toxic cynicism that psychologists refer to as "Mean World Syndrome." Mean World Syndrome is a cognitive bias where individuals perceive the world to be vastly more dangerous, selfish, and hostile than it actually is, directly due to their media consumption. When your algorithm exclusively feeds you daily examples of human cruelty, corruption, and stupidity—because that is what drives engagement—your brain recalibrates its baseline expectation of humanity.

The tragedy of the Matrix is that this psychological toll does not stay confined to our devices; it bleeds heavily into our physical reality. When you view the world through a lens of deep suspicion, you begin to treat your real-world neighbors differently. You assume bad faith. You lose the capacity to extend grace, patience, or forgiveness, subconsciously assuming that every misstep by a peer is evidence of fundamental malice. We carry the residual anxiety and aggression from our digital skirmishes to the dinner table, the workplace, and our local communities. We snap at our loved ones. We lie awake at 3 A.M., our minds racing with phantom arguments against people we have never met.

We have allowed a trillion-dollar industry to effectively hijack our emotional baselines, transforming us into chronically stressed, easily triggered, and deeply exhausted versions of ourselves.

The Outrage Machine relies entirely on breaking down our psychological resilience. But anger and fear are not the only emotions the Cartel knows how to exploit. While one side of the algorithm is busy making us furious at our enemies, the other side is quietly hard at work making us deeply insecure about ourselves. As we step away from the digital colosseum and move forward into Chapter 5, we must confront another, more silent weapon in the Cartel's arsenal: the devastating, highly profitable architecture of the Comparison Trap.

Chapter 5: The Comparison Trap

The Outrage Machine we explored in Chapter 4 relies on a loud, external explosion of emotion. But the Dopamine Cartel possesses another weapon—one that is entirely silent, deeply internal, and equally devastating. If anger is the fire that burns through the digital public square, insecurity is the invisible gas quietly filling our private spaces.

Welcome to Chapter 5: The Comparison Trap.

The human drive to evaluate our social standing is an ancient evolutionary trait. For millennia, we survived by ensuring we were valuable, accepted members of a small tribe. We looked to our immediate peers to gauge our progress, our safety, and our worth. But the Matrix has hijacked this baseline survival instinct, scaling it to a planetary level and warping it into a relentless, inescapable competition against a digital opponent that does not actually exist.

In this chapter, we will dissect the architecture of digital inadequacy. We begin by unmasking **Curated Realities and Widespread Imposter Syndrome**. The internet is not a mirror reflecting human life; it is a highly edited, heavily monetized highlight reel. We will explore the deep psychological damage that occurs when we are forced to continuously compare our messy, complex, and often mundane "behind-the-scenes" reality with the perfectly lit and algorithmically optimized "front stage" of everyone else's lives. The intended result is a generational epidemic of imposter syndrome—a pervasive, crushing belief that everyone else has figured life out while we are fundamentally failing.

Next, we shift from lifestyle comparison to the physical devastation caused by **The Perfection Algorithm: Beauty Filters and Body Image**. We will look at how the Cartel has weaponized the human form. Through the normalization of hyper-realistic augmented reality filters and the algorithm's mathematical preference for entirely unattainable physical ideals, platforms have effectively commercialized body dysmorphia. We will examine how this toxic digital environment is actively rewriting our self-perception, driving an unprecedented global surge in physical insecurity, eating disorders, and cosmetic alterations.

Finally, we will confront the psychological glue that holds this entire trap together: **Fear of Missing Out (FOMO) as a Control Mechanism**. FOMO is often brushed off as a trivial, modern anxiety—a punchline for the smartphone generation. In reality, it is a highly calibrated, deeply cynical corporate retention metric. We will uncover how the platforms intentionally engineer interfaces—such as twenty-four-hour expiring stories, live status indicators, and exclusive algorithmic trends—to manufacture an artificial sense of scarcity. They instill a constant, low-grade panic that life is happening without you, ensuring you remain tethered to the feed just to prove you still exist within the tribe.

By the end of this chapter, you will understand that your lingering feelings of inadequacy are not a personal failure. They are the highly profitable, meticulously manufactured product of a system that knows a secure, self-accepting user is terrible for business.

5.1 Curated Realities and Widespread Imposter Syndrome

To understand the specific psychological trap of the Social Media Matrix, we must first look at how human beings construct their sense of self. In 1954, psychologist Leon Festinger proposed the Social Comparison Theory. Festinger argued that humans possess an innate, biological drive to evaluate their own progress, opinions, and abilities by comparing themselves to others. For the vast majority of human history, this was a localized and highly necessary survival mechanism. You compared your harvest to your neighbor's harvest; you compared your physical strength to the other members of your tribe. You saw their successes, but crucially, you also saw their failures, their boredom, and their daily struggles. You were comparing your reality to their reality.

The Dopamine Cartel fundamentally shattered this natural equilibrium. The digital world is not a reflection of reality; it is a highly sanitized, meticulously edited, and algorithmically optimized highlight reel.

When you open a social media application, you are immediately bombarded by curated perfection. You see the flawless vacation photos, the effortless career promotions, the seemingly perfect romantic relationships, and the impeccably styled homes. What you do not see is the crushing credit card debt funding that vacation, the profound anxiety behind the career update, the bitter argument that occurred right before the couples' selfie, or the pile of laundry sitting just out of frame.

The danger lies in how our brains process this asymmetrical information. While your rational prefrontal cortex might logically understand that a photo is staged or heavily edited, your emotional limbic system processes the image as objective reality. You are constantly comparing your gritty, unedited "behind-the-scenes" life—complete with all its mundane struggles, doubts, and failures—with the polished, hyper-curated "front stage" of everyone else's lives.

Mathematically, this is a game you can never win. You are no longer comparing yourself to the fifty people in your immediate physical community; you are being force-fed the absolute top one percent of global success, beauty, and wealth, continuously surfaced by an algorithm designed to capture your attention.

The psychological fallout of this relentless, unbalanced comparison is a catastrophic rise in what was once a rare psychological phenomenon: Imposter Syndrome.

Traditionally, imposter syndrome was a term used to describe high-achieving individuals in the workplace who felt they did not deserve their success and lived in fear of being exposed as a "fraud." Today, the Matrix has democratized this neurosis, scaling it to a planetary level and applying it not just to careers, but to human existence itself. We are living through an epidemic of existential imposter syndrome.

Because the algorithm overwhelmingly rewards positive, aspirational content with higher visibility and "likes," users are socially conditioned to hide their struggles. Vulnerability is algorithmically punished; perfection is rewarded. This creates a silent, collective agreement among billions of users to maintain a facade of constant happiness and success. Consequently, when a user inevitably experiences natural human suffering—sadness, failure, loneliness, or stagnation—they look at their feed and falsely conclude that they are the only one struggling. The curated reality of the Matrix convinces them that everyone else has figured life out, and they alone are failing at being a functional human being.

This pervasive sense of inadequacy is not an accidental byproduct of social media; it is an incredibly lucrative emotional state.

The Dopamine Cartel operates on an economic model that requires constant consumption. A user who is deeply secure, contented, and at peace with their life is a terrible consumer. They do not need to buy products to fill an emotional void. However, a user who is trapped in a cycle of upward social comparison, paralyzed by imposter syndrome, and terrified that they are falling behind their peers is the perfect target for advertisers.

When you feel inadequate, you are biologically primed to seek a solution to restore your social standing. The Matrix ingeniously provides the poison and then sells you the cure. Right beneath the post that triggered your feelings of professional inadequacy is an advertisement for an expensive online masterclass. Right beneath the photo that made you feel insecure about your home is a targeted ad for luxury furniture. The Cartel manufactures your insecurity through curated realities, and then auctions off your desperation to the highest bidding advertiser.

We are sacrificing our internal peace on the altar of external validation, frantically polishing our digital avatars while our actual mental health deteriorates in the shadows. We are chasing a mirage engineered to keep us scrolling and spending. And as we will discover in the next section, this demand for curated perfection does not just warp our perception of our lives and careers; it is systematically destroying our relationship with our own physical bodies.

5.2 The Perfection Algorithm: Beauty Filters and Body Image

In the early days of social media, digital photo manipulation was a complex skill reserved for professional graphic designers using expensive software. Today, it is a frictionless, automated process executed in a fraction of a second by artificial intelligence. We have transitioned from comparing our raw, unfiltered lives to a curated highlight reel, to comparing our actual, physical flesh to mathematically impossible digital avatars. This is the weaponization of the human form, and it operates through a devastating piece of code: the Perfection Algorithm.

To understand how this happened, we must look at the rapid evolution of Augmented Reality (AR) filters. When facial filters were first introduced to the Matrix, they were largely marketed as playful, harmless gimmicks—digital dog ears, oversized glasses, or cartoonish voice changers. But as the underlying machine learning technology grew exponentially more sophisticated, the objective shifted from entertainment to augmentation. The new generation of beauty filters does not add playful graphics; it acts as an invisible, instantaneous digital scalpel.

With a single tap, these filters eradicate pores, smooth out skin textures, whiten teeth, enlarge eyes, plump lips, and physically alter bone structure to slim the jawline and raise the cheekbones. The danger lies in their hyper-realism. Unlike obvious Photoshop jobs of the past, these AR filters map seamlessly onto the human face in real-time, even adjusting perfectly as the user moves and speaks on video. The resulting image looks completely authentic, effectively blurring the line between physical reality and digital manipulation.

However, these filters are not neutral. They are governed by an algorithm that has been explicitly trained on a highly specific, often Eurocentric, and mathematically synthesized standard of beauty. The Perfection Algorithm dictates that only one type of face is truly valuable within the

Attention Economy. When millions of users apply these exact same standardized filters, it creates a terrifying homogenization of beauty. We are no longer celebrating diverse human features; we are conforming to a singular, machine-generated template.

Furthermore, the algorithm financially rewards this conformity. Social media platforms prioritize engagement above all else, and through billions of data points, the algorithm has learned that faces adhering to this synthetic standard generate higher metrics—more dwell time, more likes, and more followers. Therefore, if a user posts a raw, unfiltered photo, the algorithm quietly suppresses its reach. If that same user applies a beauty filter, the algorithm artificially inflates their visibility, pushing them to the top of the feed. The Matrix essentially holds a user's social capital hostage, demanding digital cosmetic surgery as the price of admission to the public square.

The psychological toll of this system is catastrophic, particularly for the youth target demographic. We are currently witnessing an unprecedented spike in body dysmorphia, a severe psychological condition characterized by an obsessive focus on perceived flaws in physical appearance. Mental health professionals have coined a new term for this specific digital affliction: "Snapchat Dysmorphia." Historically, patients seeking cosmetic surgery would bring photographs of celebrities to their doctors. Today, patients are bringing heavily filtered selfies of themselves, desperately asking medical professionals to make them look like their own impossible digital avatars.

This creates a profound and deeply painful dissociation. When a user spends hours staring at a flawless, algorithmically optimized version of themselves on a screen, the inevitable return to the physical mirror becomes a traumatic event. The reflection in the glass—with its natural asymmetry, pores, and blemishes—is no longer recognized as normal; it is perceived as a grotesque failure. The brain cannot reconcile the physical reality with the digital persona, leading to crushing physical insecurity, social withdrawal, and a surge in eating disorders.

Once again, we must follow the money to understand why this architecture of insecurity is permitted to thrive. The Dopamine Cartel does not enforce these beauty standards out of aesthetic preference; they do it because physical insecurity is a multi-billion-dollar industry. A user who is completely comfortable in their own skin is a commercial dead end. But a user who has been algorithmically conditioned to despise their natural face and body is the perfect, highly vulnerable target for a massive ecosystem of advertisers.

The platform engineers the insecurity through the Perfection Algorithm, and then seamlessly serves up targeted advertisements for diet suppressants, teeth whiteners, anti-aging serums, and cosmetic procedures. They break the mirror, and then charge you by the minute to rent the tape to fix it.

We have allowed a corporate syndicate to fundamentally rewrite the definition of human beauty, turning our own faces into a battleground for engagement and profit. Yet, as we will explore in the next section, the Matrix does not just want you to feel insecure about how you look; it wants you to be terrified about what you might be missing.

5.3 Fear of Missing Out (FOMO) as a Control Mechanism

In modern pop culture, the "Fear of Missing Out," or FOMO, is often treated as a mild, somewhat humorous millennial affliction. It is the punchline of a joke when you decide to stay home on a Friday night instead of going to a party, or the hashtag used when you see friends vacationing without you. But inside the glass-walled conference rooms of the Dopamine Cartel, FOMO is not a joke. It is not a trivial anxiety. It is a highly calibrated, meticulously engineered, and aggressively monitored corporate retention metric. It is the psychological glue that holds the entire Comparison Trap together.

To understand how FOMO was weaponized, we must again look to our evolutionary past. For prehistoric humans, missing out was not a matter of social inconvenience; it was a matter of life and death. If the tribe discovered a new water source, moved the camp, or learned of a nearby predator, and you were not present to receive that information, your chances of survival plummeted to zero. The human nervous system evolved to treat social exclusion and information deficits as literal, physical threats. The agonizing pang of anxiety you feel when you realize you have been left out of a loop is your ancient brain screaming at you to rejoin the safety of the herd.

The architects of the Social Media Matrix understood that they could not rely solely on users *wanting* to open their apps. Desire is fleeting; a user might find something more productive to do. To guarantee the astronomical daily active user (DAU) numbers required by their shareholders, the Cartel had to make users absolutely terrified of *not* opening their apps. They had to manufacture a perpetual state of artificial scarcity.

The most blatant manifestation of this strategy was the invention of ephemeral content—specifically, the "Story" format. In the early days of social media, content was posted to a permanent grid. If you did not log on for three days, you could simply scroll down and catch up. The user was in control of the timeline. The "Story" feature obliterated that control by introducing a twenty-four-hour self-destruct timer.

This seemingly simple UI update was a masterpiece of behavioral manipulation. By placing a ticking clock on social interactions, the platform created a manufactured crisis. If you do not look at the content right now, it will be gone forever, and you will be permanently excluded from the shared cultural moment. It forces the user to check the application obsessively, not because they are expecting something good, but because they are terrified of missing something entirely unknown. It is a hostage tactic for human attention, transforming the act of logging on from a leisure activity into a biological obligation.

This control mechanism extends deeply into the messaging infrastructures we use daily. Consider the subtle, ubiquitous status indicators: the green dot indicating a friend is "active now," the timestamp of when they were "last seen," the read receipts confirming a message was opened, and the animated ellipses indicating someone is currently typing.

We are told these features exist for our convenience, to make digital communication feel more seamless and alive. In reality, they are psychological tethers designed to induce a constant, low-grade panic. They create an invisible, implied social contract of instant availability. When you turn your phone off, you are not just taking a break; you are actively, publicly severing the tether. You know that your peers can see your absence. The Matrix makes the act of disconnecting feel like an aggressive act of social withdrawal, thereby punishing you with anxiety the moment you try to step away.

Furthermore, the algorithm accelerates the speed of cultural relevance to an impossible velocity. Inside the echo chambers, outrage cycles, viral trends, and internal memes rise and burn out in a matter of hours. If you decide to take a digital detox for a single weekend, you return on Monday feeling like an alien who has lost the ability to speak the local language. You are socially penalized for resting. The sheer volume and speed of the information stream ensure that you always feel slightly behind, slightly out of touch, and desperate to catch up.

The psychological toll of this constant vigilance is exhausting. It is the reason millions of people suffer from "phantom vibration syndrome"—the hallucination that their phone is buzzing in their pocket when it isn't. It is the reason we instinctively reach for a glowing screen in the middle of the night, our sleep cycles shattered by the subconscious fear that the digital tribe has moved on without us in the dark.

The Comparison Trap is a three-pronged assault on human security. The Cartel curates an impossible reality that makes you feel like an imposter in your own life. They deploy the Perfection Algorithm to make you despise your own physical reflection. And finally, they engineer FOMO to ensure that no matter how inadequate and exhausted you feel, you are far too terrified to ever look away.

Once your self-worth has been sufficiently eroded and your nervous system is trapped in a permanent state of anxious vigilance, you lose the cognitive bandwidth required to do anything else. You lose the ability to read a book, master a complex skill, or sit quietly with your own thoughts. And that brings us to the next great casualty of the Matrix: the deliberate, systematic destruction of our capacity for deep work.

Chapter 6: The Erosion of Deep Work

The previous chapters detailed how the Dopamine Cartel hijacks our emotions—sparking outrage to fuel engagement and seeding deep insecurity to drive continuous consumption. But to maintain total control over your digital habits, the Matrix requires more than just the manipulation of your feelings. It requires the deliberate, systematic dismantling of your cognitive focus.

Welcome to Chapter 6: The Erosion of Deep Work.

The ability to concentrate intensely on a single, demanding task without distraction is the foundation of all meaningful human achievement. From monumental scientific breakthroughs and artistic masterpieces to the quiet, vital act of simply being fully present with a loved one, our greatest triumphs require unbroken focus. The Cartel understands this perfectly. They know that a mind capable of deep work is a mind that is self-sufficient. Deep work requires patience, extended isolation, and a high tolerance for temporary boredom—all biological states that generate absolutely zero in advertising revenue. Therefore, they have engineered a digital environment where sustained attention is mathematically nearly impossible.

We begin this chapter by completely dismantling one of the most pervasive and destructive lies of the modern era in **The Dangerous Myth of Multitasking**. For the last decade, we have been aggressively conditioned by technology companies to wear our divided attention as a badge of honor. We proudly juggle incoming emails, dozens of open browser tabs, and vibrating group chats, falsely believing we are maximizing our daily productivity. We will look at the hard neuroscience proving that the human brain is fundamentally incapable of processing simultaneous, high-level cognitive tasks. What the Matrix sells as multitasking is actually rapid task-switching, a highly inefficient neurological glitch designed to keep us chronically engaged but perpetually unaccomplished.

Next, we will examine the severe biological and mental cost of this intentionally fractured existence in **Context Switching and Severe Cognitive Fatigue**. Every time your device pings and you shift your gaze from your primary work to a glowing screen, your brain is forced to pay a heavy metabolic tax. We will explore the phenomenon of "attention residue"—how even a fleeting, three-second glance at a notification can entirely derail a complex train of thought for up to twenty minutes. This constant, forced shifting clouds our judgment, smothers our creativity, and plunges us into a state of profound mental exhaustion. We are not just losing minutes to our devices; we are actively burning out our cognitive hardware.

However, this chapter is not merely a diagnosis of our collective, modern brain fog; it is a tactical manual for your intellectual recovery. In the final section, we pivot from the problem to the solution, outlining practical **Strategies for Reclaiming Your Attention Span**. We will provide actionable frameworks to protect your limited cognitive bandwidth, from establishing rigid digital boundaries and single-tasking disciplines to fundamentally rewiring your brain's baseline tolerance for silence.

By the end of this chapter, you will understand that reclaiming your attention is not just a productivity hack. It is an act of profound, necessary rebellion against a trillion-dollar industry designed to keep you shallow, scattered, and endlessly scrolling.

6.1 The Dangerous Myth of Multitasking

For the past two decades, the modern corporate world and the tech industry have aggressively promoted a highly specific, deeply toxic archetype of the ideal worker: the master multitasker. We are constantly conditioned to view divided attention as a badge of honor. The image of the hyper-productive digital citizen is someone who can flawlessly answer an email, participate in a video conference, monitor a group chat, and scroll through a news feed simultaneously. We proudly list "excellent multitasking skills" on our professional resumes. We believe that by doing three things at once, we are effectively tripling our output and conquering the demands of the information age. We view the singular, unbroken focus of previous generations as an outdated relic of the analog past, completely unsuited for the relentless speed of modern life.

There is only one problem with this prevailing cultural narrative: it is a complete neurological fiction.

Cognitive neuroscientists are unequivocally clear on this matter: the human brain is fundamentally incapable of processing simultaneous, high-level cognitive tasks. When we think we are multitasking, we are actually engaging in a biological phenomenon known as "rapid task-switching." Your brain cannot write a coherent email and actively listen to a complex conference call at the exact same time. Instead, your prefrontal cortex—the command center for logical thought, decision-making, and focus—is frantically toggling back and forth between the two tasks. It acts like a panicked spotlight operator trying to illuminate two different, widely separated stages in the dark.

This toggle happens in a fraction of a second, which creates a powerful, persistent illusion of simultaneous execution. But it is an illusion that comes with a devastating biological tax. Every single time your brain shifts its focus from one stimulus to another, it must engage in a complex neurological reset. It has to entirely disengage from the rules and context of the first task, activate the rules and context of the second task, and attempt to recall exactly where it left off.

This invisible neurological shuffling is not free. It consumes massive amounts of oxygenated glucose, the very fuel your brain requires to think clearly and regulate emotions. When you spend your day rapidly toggling between browser tabs, glowing notifications, and incoming messages, you are effectively redlining your brain's metabolic engine. This is exactly why you can sit in an ergonomic office chair for eight hours, staring at a screen, and log off feeling profoundly, physically exhausted, despite having accomplished very little of substance. You have burned through your daily reserve of cognitive energy simply managing the chaotic transitions between tasks, rather than deeply executing the tasks themselves.

The most insidious aspect of the multitasking myth is that it actually *feels* incredibly productive. When you rapidly clear your inbox while listening to a podcast and glancing at a social feed, your brain's dopamine pathways light up. You feel a sudden rush of accomplishment because you are crossing multiple micro-tasks off a list in rapid succession. The Cartel's engineers know that our brains love the instant gratification of completing small, easy tasks. But this is a chemical deception. You are mistaking the friction of rapid movement for the momentum of actual progress. You are successfully completing a dozen trivial tasks, while the one deep, meaningful project that requires your full intellectual capacity remains untouched.

Why, then, is the myth of multitasking so relentlessly pushed by the architecture of our devices? Because deep, unbroken focus is the absolute enemy of the Attention Economy.

If you sit down to read a challenging book, write a complex piece of code, or engage in a deeply focused conversation, you are functionally useless to the Dopamine Cartel. You are not generating behavioral data, you are not triggering intermittent variable rewards, and you are not viewing advertisements. Deep work requires a closed system. The Cartel's trillion-dollar business model requires an open system. They need you to believe that checking a notification while writing a report is not a disruption, but a necessary act of modern efficiency. By convincing you that you can successfully do both, they give themselves permission to constantly interrupt you.

The cost of this manufactured distraction is measured in the catastrophic decline of our output. Studies conducted by leading research universities have shown that heavy multitaskers are actually worse at filtering out irrelevant information than those who focus on one task at a time. The constant bombardment of stimuli actively degrades the brain's working memory. Furthermore, research has demonstrated that engaging in rapid task-switching during a complex cognitive assignment temporarily drops a person's effective IQ by up to ten points. This is a cognitive decline roughly equivalent to losing an entire night of sleep, or being legally intoxicated.

You would never knowingly attempt to build a meaningful project while entirely sleep-deprived. Yet, by submitting to the relentless pings and pop-ups of the Matrix, we voluntarily induce that exact state of cognitive impairment every single day. We have allowed the architects of the Cartel to convince us that our minds are computer processors, capable of running multiple high-demand applications simultaneously. But we are not machines. And as we will discover in the next section, the violent, constant shifting of our attention leaves a lingering, toxic residue that actively poisons our ability to think deeply long after the screen goes dark.

6.2 Context Switching and Severe Cognitive Fatigue

Imagine you are driving a car at highway speeds. Suddenly, you throw the transmission into reverse, immediately slam it back into drive, and attempt to accelerate again. You do not need to be a mechanic to understand that performing this action repeatedly will rapidly destroy the engine. Yet, this violent, grinding gear-shift is precisely what we force our brains to endure hundreds of times a day. In the realm of cognitive science, this destructive maneuver is known as "context switching," and it is the primary reason an entire generation is currently suffering from unprecedented levels of severe cognitive fatigue.

To understand the damage, we must examine the anatomy of an interruption. When you are engaged in a complex task—writing a proposal, studying for an exam, or having a meaningful conversation—your brain constructs a highly intricate cognitive architecture. It loads the relevant facts, rules, and emotional context into your working memory, essentially building a fragile, invisible scaffolding to support your deep thought.

Then, your phone vibrates.

You break your focus and glance at the screen. It is an email from a frustrated client, or a breaking news alert about a political crisis. In that microscopic fraction of a second, the scaffolding collapses. Your brain must instantly dump the context of your deep work and load the entirely new, highly stressful context of the notification. You read the message, put the phone face down, and attempt to return to your original task. You tell yourself that the interruption only took three seconds, so it cost you nothing.

You are entirely wrong.

You have just fallen victim to a phenomenon that organizational psychologists call "attention residue." When you switch your gaze from the notification back to your work, your cognitive focus does not cleanly follow you. A significant portion of your brain's processing power remains stuck on the previous task. Your eyes might be looking at the spreadsheet in front of you, but a heavy residue of your attention is still lingering on the frustrated client or the political crisis. You are attempting to do deep work with a compromised, fragmented mind.

The mathematics of this fragmentation are staggering. Research conducted by cognitive scientists at the University of California, Irvine, revealed that after a single interruption, it takes the human brain an average of twenty-three minutes and fifteen seconds to fully rebuild that invisible scaffolding and return to a state of deep, unbroken focus.

Now, apply that math to your daily life. If you check your phone, reply to a message, or glance at an inbox just once every twenty minutes, you are mathematically guaranteeing that you will never experience a single moment of deep focus throughout your entire day. You are perpetually living in the shallow end of your own intellectual capacity, constantly recovering from the last interruption just in time to be derailed by the next.

This perpetual state of recovery extracts a devastating biological toll. The human brain, despite accounting for only about two percent of our body weight, consumes a massive twenty percent of our daily energy. The prefrontal cortex, which governs deep focus, is an absolute glutton for oxygenated glucose. Every time you force a context switch, your brain has to burn an enormous amount of metabolic fuel to tear down one cognitive environment and build another.

This relentless metabolic drain is the biological root of modern cognitive fatigue. It explains why you can spend eight hours sitting perfectly still in a comfortable chair, doing nothing more physically demanding than typing on a keyboard, and finish the day feeling profoundly, completely exhausted. Your muscles are not tired; your battery is simply dead. You have burned through your daily reserve of intellectual fuel merely managing the chaotic transitions between digital inputs, leaving absolutely no energy for actual, meaningful creation.

The Dopamine Cartel is intimately aware of this metabolic tax, but they do not view it as a problem. In fact, it is a feature of their design. The social media feed itself is the ultimate engine of context switching. When you scroll, you are forced to aggressively shift your emotional and cognitive context every three seconds. You swipe from a devastating news story about a natural disaster, to a video of a comedian, to a targeted advertisement for running shoes, to a photograph of your friend's newborn baby. The brain is violently whipped back and forth across wildly different emotional spectrums.

This engineered chaos keeps the brain in a shallow, highly reactive state of high arousal. It systematically destroys your capacity for linear, contemplative thought. When your mind is thoroughly exhausted from endless context switching, your prefrontal cortex essentially powers down. You lose the willpower required to close the app, put down the device, and engage in something difficult or restorative. You default to the path of least resistance, which is to simply keep scrolling.

Severe cognitive fatigue is not a sign of personal weakness, nor is it a natural consequence of aging. It is the intended outcome of a digital environment that treats human attention like an infinite resource to be strip-mined. By normalizing constant interruption, the Matrix keeps us too exhausted to build our own lives, ensuring we have just enough energy left to passively consume theirs.

6.3 Strategies for Reclaiming Your Attention Span

Understanding the biological mechanics of cognitive fatigue is only half the battle. Diagnosis without treatment is merely despair. If the Dopamine

Cartel has engineered our environment to systematically strip-mine our attention, then the act of reclaiming our focus is not a matter of trying harder; it is a matter of structural, environmental rebellion. You cannot out-willpower a trillion-dollar supercomputer operating on principles of advanced behavioral psychology. But you can outsmart it by fundamentally changing the rules of engagement. Reclaiming your attention span requires treating your cognitive bandwidth as a fiercely protected, finite resource. Here are the foundational strategies for breaking the cycle of constant interruption and rebuilding your capacity for deep work.

Strategy 1: Reintroducing Architectural Friction

The Cartel's primary weapon is the eradication of friction. They made consumption entirely effortless, removing stopping cues and boundaries. Your first line of defense is to ruthlessly reintroduce friction into your digital environment.

This begins with an aggressive, uncompromising audit of your notifications. Every single ping, banner, and vibration is a non-consensual demand for your attention. Turn them all off, with the strict exception of direct communication from vital human beings. A social media platform does not need the ability to tap you on the shoulder. Next, alter the physical appearance of your digital environment. Switch your smartphone screen to grayscale. The Matrix relies on hyper-stimulating, casino-style colors (especially the red notification badge) to trigger dopamine; grayscale renders the infinite scroll incredibly dull, breaking the visual, chemical spell.

Furthermore, you must establish physical boundaries. The most effective way to prevent context switching during deep work is to ensure the device is not in the same room as you. If your phone is within arm's reach, even if it is turned face down, your brain is still dedicating background processing power to the possibility of checking it. Put the phone in a drawer, in another room, or utilize timed lockboxes. Force yourself to physically stand up and walk to the device if you genuinely need it. By making the act of distraction physically difficult, you give your prefrontal cortex the necessary seconds to wake up and intercept the impulse.

Strategy 2: The Discipline of Single-Tasking

Once you have secured your environment, you must actively rehabilitate your fractured cognitive hardware. Years of rapid task-switching have essentially trained your brain to panic in the absence of constant, varied stimulation. You must relearn the lost art of single-tasking.

This requires structured, rigid boundaries around your time. Implement ruthless time-blocking, dedicating specific, non-negotiable windows of your day exclusively to one task. When you enter a deep work block, you must close every irrelevant browser tab. Put your device on airplane mode or use website blockers to sever your internet connection entirely. If you are writing, you only write. If you are reading, you only read.

Initially, this will feel agonizing. Your brain, starved of its usual dopamine drips, will scream at you to check your inbox, glance at the news, or find a distraction. You must push through this cognitive withdrawal. Start with incredibly small intervals—just fifteen to twenty minutes of unbroken focus using methods like the Pomodoro technique—and slowly build the muscle back. Over time, the anxiety of missing out will fade, replaced by the profound, quiet satisfaction of genuine immersion and high-level execution.

Strategy 3: Embracing Boredom and the Default Mode Network

The final, and perhaps most difficult, strategy is learning to embrace boredom. The Matrix has conditioned us to view any moment of stillness—waiting in a line, sitting on a bus, or folding laundry—as a void that must be instantly filled with digital consumption. We have entirely lost the capacity to just *be*.

But cognitive science tells us that these moments of idle boredom are not wasted time; they are vital neurological recovery periods. When your brain is unfocused and not consuming external information, it activates the "default mode network." This is the background processing state where your mind consolidates memories, processes complex emotions, connects disparate ideas, and generates creative insights. By constantly reaching for a digital pacifier the second we feel a pang of boredom, we are suffocating our own creativity and emotional regulation.

You must actively practice doing nothing. Leave your phone at home when you go for a walk. Stare out of a window. Allow your mind to wander without a digital tether. You are not losing time; you are letting your cognitive engine cool down and perform necessary internal maintenance.

Reclaiming your attention span is not a one-time life hack; it is a daily, deliberate practice of self-defense. It is the conscious decision to stop treating your mind as a public thoroughfare for corporate advertisers and start treating it as a private sanctuary. When you successfully rebuild your capacity for deep work, you do not just become more productive; you regain your autonomy.

But as we fortify our own minds, we must turn our attention to those who are entirely defenseless against this architecture. The adults who built the Matrix were old enough to remember a world before it existed. The next generation is not so lucky. As we move into Chapter 7, we will examine the most devastating and morally bankrupt facet of the Dopamine Cartel: the deliberate targeting and hijacking of the vulnerable, developing brain.

CHAPTER 7: THE YOUTH TARGET

If the adults who designed the Social Media Matrix are struggling to maintain their cognitive autonomy, what hope does a child have? The previous chapters mapped the devastating impact of the Attention Economy on the mature human brain. But there is a darker, more cynical layer to this corporate enterprise. The adults who built the Cartel, and those of us who first logged onto its platforms, remember a world before the digital cage existed. We have an analog baseline to fall back on. The next generation does not. They are the first humans in history to be born entirely inside the Matrix.

Welcome to Chapter 7: The Youth Target.

This chapter confronts the most morally bankrupt facet of the Dopamine Cartel: the deliberate, calculated exploitation of children and adolescents. We will begin by examining the grim biology of this exploitation in **Hijacking the Vulnerable Developing Brain**. The human prefrontal cortex—the region of the brain responsible for impulse control, long-term planning, and emotional regulation—does not fully mature until our mid-twenties. The Cartel's engineers are intimately aware of this developmental gap. They have designed their algorithms to relentlessly exploit a teenager's hyper-sensitive limbic system, weaponizing their desperate biological need for peer approval and social validation. We will explore how treating a thirteen-year-old's brain as a raw, monetizable commodity is not a design flaw, but the digital equivalent of the tobacco industry intentionally targeting minors to secure lifetime customers.

Next, we will look at how this hijacked biology plays out in the real world in **Cyberbullying and the 24/7 Social Pressure Cooker**. For previous generations, the social brutalization of middle and high school had a physical boundary. When the school bell rang, you went home. Your bedroom was a sanctuary. The Matrix has entirely eradicated that sanctuary. We will uncover how the Cartel has transformed modern adolescence into a relentless, twenty-four-hour performance, trapping youth in a digital panopticon where bullying, exclusion, and peer pressure follow them into their beds. The natural cruelty of childhood has been digitized, algorithmically amplified, and made terrifyingly permanent.

Finally, we will examine the catastrophic societal fallout in **The Rise of Screen-Induced Anxiety in the Next Generation**. We are currently witnessing an unprecedented, global collapse in youth mental health. We will connect the data between the skyrocketing rates of teen depression, clinical anxiety, and self-harm directly to the deployment of the infinite scroll, beauty filters, and algorithmic outrage. We will look at how a generation raised on a diet of artificial scarcity and curated perfection is crumbling under the weight of a virtual world they were never neurologically equipped to carry.

By the end of this chapter, the narrative that social media is simply a harmless, modern "rite of passage" will be destroyed. You will see it as a highly orchestrated, multi-billion-dollar predatory system, and you will understand exactly why we must aggressively intervene to pull the youth out of the Matrix.

7.1 Hijacking the Vulnerable Developing Brain

To comprehend the true moral bankruptcy of the Dopamine Cartel, we must first abandon a widespread, dangerous misconception. We often view teenagers as simply miniature, inexperienced adults—individuals who possess the same fundamental cognitive machinery as we do, but who merely lack the discipline or willpower to put their phones down. This is biologically false. From a neurological standpoint, human adolescence is a period of massive, chaotic architectural reconstruction. The teenage brain is not fully built; it is a construction site. And the engineers of the Matrix have intentionally set up shop right in the middle of it.

To understand how this hijacking occurs, we must look at the specific, asymmetrical way the human brain develops. Brain maturation generally occurs from the back to the front. The first area to fully mature during early adolescence is the limbic system. Located deep within the brain, this ancient neural network is the engine of emotion, risk-taking, and the intense pursuit of social reward and dopamine. It is highly reactive and immensely powerful.

Meanwhile, the prefrontal cortex—the region located right behind the forehead—is notoriously late to the party. This is the brain's rational command center. It is responsible for impulse control, complex decision-making, evaluating long-term consequences, and regulating intense emotions. The prefrontal cortex does not finish fully wiring itself until a person reaches their mid-twenties.

This creates a terrifying, decade-long biological gap. Cognitive scientists often describe the teenage brain as a high-performance sports car equipped with a massive, highly sensitive accelerator (the limbic system) but completely missing the brakes (the prefrontal cortex).

For millions of years, this temporary imbalance served a crucial evolutionary purpose. The hypersensitive limbic system propelled young humans to break away from the safety of their parents, take risks, and form the essential peer bonds necessary for survival and reproduction. For a teenager, social acceptance is not merely a preference; their developing brain processes peer approval as a literal matter of life and death. If the ancient tribe rejected you, you perished.

The architects of the Social Media Matrix do not view this neurological gap as a developmental vulnerability to be protected. They view it as a highly lucrative attack vector.

When a teenager logs onto a social platform, the algorithm flawlessly targets this exact biological imperative. The Cartel took the messy, subjective, and vital process of adolescent social bonding and reduced it to a cold, quantified metric of "likes," "views," and "followers." Because the teenage limbic system is desperately scanning the environment for any sign of social standing, it latches onto these metrics with terrifying intensity. A single notification ping delivers a potent, concentrated hit of dopamine directly to a brain that is biologically desperate for it.

But crucially, because the prefrontal cortex is offline, the teenager lacks the neurological defense mechanisms required to regulate this dopamine loop. An adult might receive ten "likes" on a photo, feel a brief moment of satisfaction, and then rationally put the phone in their pocket to go cook dinner. The adult's prefrontal cortex successfully applies the brakes. A thirteen-year-old possesses no such brakes. Their brain demands they stay on the app, constantly refreshing the feed, terrified that if they look away, their social status will plummet. They are biologically defenseless against the slot-machine mechanics we explored in Chapter 1.

This exploitation is not a tragic accident of the digital age; it is a calculated, predatory business model that mirrors the darkest chapters of corporate history. Just as the tobacco industry once deployed cartoon mascots, flavored cigarettes, and aggressive youth marketing to hook a demographic lacking the maturity to assess long-term health risks, the Dopamine Cartel utilizes gamification, augmented reality beauty filters, and infinite scrolling to capture the youth. They know that if they can successfully rewire a user's neural pathways during their most plastic, developmental years, they have secured a guaranteed, lifelong consumer.

It is an entirely asymmetrical war. On one side of the screen is a vulnerable, developing human brain, desperately trying to figure out its place in the world. On the other side of the screen is a trillion-dollar supercomputer, programmed by thousands of behavioral psychologists, running millions of algorithmic tests a second, specifically designed to exploit that child's deepest evolutionary insecurities.

When a teenager struggles to put their device away at two in the morning, sacrificing their sleep to monitor a group chat or obsessively check the view count on a video, they are not exhibiting a moral failing. They are not simply "misbehaving." They are being successfully conquered.

This constant, metricized hijack of the adolescent brain sets the stage for a waking nightmare. Because as the algorithm forces these vulnerable minds into a perpetual, high-stakes competition for social survival, it fundamentally warps how they treat one another. As we turn to the next section, we will see what happens when the natural cruelty of childhood is digitized, amplified, and made terrifyingly permanent inside the Matrix.

7.2 Cyberbullying and the 24/7 Social Pressure Cooker

For generations, the social cruelty of adolescence was a geographically contained phenomenon. If a child was bullied, ostracized, or humiliated, the trauma was generally confined to the physical boundaries of the schoolyard, the locker room, or the cafeteria. When the final bell rang at three o'clock, the child was granted a biological and psychological reprieve. They could go home, close their bedroom door, and temporarily escape the vicious hierarchy of their peers. The home served as an absolute sanctuary. The Dopamine Cartel has effectively bulldozed the walls of that sanctuary. Today, the smartphone in a teenager's pocket guarantees that the bullies follow them home, walk through the front door, and sit with them on their bed.

We have trapped the next generation inside a 24/7 Social Pressure Cooker. To survive adolescence in the digital age requires managing a relentless, high-stakes public relations campaign. Teenagers are no longer simply communicating with their friends; they are actively managing a personal brand before an audience of hundreds, or even thousands, of their peers. The Matrix demands constant availability and flawless curation. Through the weaponization of read receipts, typing indicators, and real-time location tracking features like Snap Maps, a teenager can never truly clock out of their social life. If they do not respond to a message immediately, their absence is broadcasted. If they choose to stay home on a Friday night, they can physically watch the avatars of their peers congregating without them on a digital map. The pressure to perform, to react, and to remain visible is crushing, and it never, ever stops.

This constant connectivity has fundamentally mutated the nature of adolescent cruelty, birthing a highly efficient, digitized strain of abuse:

cyberbullying. The Cartel did not invent bullying, but they built the ultimate infrastructure for its amplification. In the physical world, bullying requires direct confrontation, which naturally limits its frequency. But behind the cold glass of a screen, the "online disinhibition effect" takes hold. Because the attacker does not have to see the immediate, painful reaction on their victim's face, empathy is completely bypassed. The cruelty becomes abstract, allowing children to inflict a level of psychological violence on one another that they would never possess the audacity to deliver in person.

Furthermore, the algorithms actively pour gasoline on this cruelty because drama and conflict are the ultimate drivers of engagement. When a vicious rumor, an embarrassing photograph, or a cruel video is posted, it does not just reach a few kids in a hallway; it can reach the entire school district in a matter of minutes. The algorithm detects the sudden spike in comments, shares, and dwell time, and artificially inflates the post's visibility. The Cartel's machinery does not differentiate between a viral dance trend and a digital public execution; it only recognizes highly profitable human attention.

But the most devastating aspect of cyberbullying is its permanence and its metricization. In the past, a cruel whisper faded into the air. In the Matrix, the cruelty is logged in a permanent digital ledger. The victim is forced to watch, in real-time, as the abuse is quantified. They see exactly how many people "liked" the cruel comment. They can see exactly how many of their peers viewed the humiliating video. The Matrix effectively crowdsources the bullying, turning peer destruction into a spectator sport where the victim's social execution is publicly scored. This metricization creates an isolating, inescapable trauma. There is no moving to a new school to escape a bad reputation when the digital ledger follows you everywhere, permanently tethered to your name.

We are forcing children to navigate a digital panopticon where their every misstep is recorded, scrutinized, and weaponized by their peers, all while the platform extracts advertising revenue from the resulting chaos. The human nervous system, especially one that is still deep in the developmental stages of adolescence, cannot sustain this level of chronic hyper-vigilance. The biological alarm bells are ringing constantly, warning the teenager that their social standing—and therefore their survival—is under imminent threat. They are trapped in a state of perpetual fight-or-flight, terrified to look at their screens, yet utterly unable to look away.

When you combine the biological vulnerability of a hijacked limbic system with the inescapable, metricized cruelty of the 24/7 pressure cooker, a psychological collapse is mathematically inevitable. The Matrix has stripped away the necessary quiet of childhood and replaced it with a digital warzone. The consequences of this environmental shift are no longer theoretical; they are manifesting in hospitals and therapy offices around the globe. As we transition to the final section of this chapter, we must confront the devastating statistical reality of what this system is actively doing to the mental health of our youth.

7.3 The Rise of Screen-Induced Anxiety in the Next Generation

For decades, psychological data tracking the mental well-being of adolescents remained relatively stable. There were natural fluctuations, but the baseline of teenage happiness, depression, and anxiety followed predictable historical patterns. Then, around the early 2010s, something unprecedented happened. Across nearly every developed nation, the data lines on adolescent mental health charts suddenly snapped upward, creating steep, terrifying hockey-stick curves. Rates of clinical anxiety, major depressive episodes, and self-harm among teenagers skyrocketed. Researchers, sociologists, and parents scrambled for an explanation, looking for a sudden economic collapse or a global geopolitical crisis. But the true catalyst was not a macro-economic event; it was the mass adoption of the smartphone and the rapid integration of the Social Media Matrix into the pockets of the youth.

We are currently witnessing the psychological collapse of a generation, driven by a pervasive, modern affliction that can only be classified as screen-induced anxiety. This is not the standard, hormonal angst that has accompanied adolescence since the dawn of time. Teenage angst is a natural friction caused by growing up. Screen-induced anxiety is a clinical, chronic state of hyper-arousal manufactured by a digital ecosystem that never allows the developing brain to rest.

To understand the mechanics of this anxiety, we must look at what the screen fundamentally displaces. The Attention Economy operates as a zero-sum game. Every hour a teenager spends endlessly scrolling, monitoring their metrics, and navigating the 24/7 Social Pressure Cooker is an hour stolen from the biological processes required to build a resilient mind.

The most devastating of these thefts is the destruction of adolescent sleep. Sleep is not a luxury for a developing brain; it is the critical maintenance window where the prefrontal cortex consolidates memories, processes emotional trauma, and resets the nervous system. Yet, the Cartel intentionally designed features like infinite scroll and auto-play to conquer the bedroom. Driven by the manufactured terror of FOMO, teenagers are sleeping with their devices beneath their pillows, their circadian rhythms shattered by blue light and the intermittent vibrations of late-night notifications. A brain deprived of sleep is a brain highly susceptible to clinical anxiety. The Matrix keeps them awake to harvest their data, leaving them neurologically defenseless the next morning.

Furthermore, the Matrix has systematically displaced the traditional, analog buffer against anxiety: unstructured, physical play. Historically, children and teenagers processed stress, learned conflict resolution, and built emotional resilience by interacting in physical spaces away from the constant supervision and judgment of the wider world. The screen has devoured that physical space. Instead of riding bikes, hanging out in basements, or playing in parks, their social lives have been entirely uploaded to a digital colosseum where every interaction is public, permanent, and algorithmically scored. When you remove physical play and replace it with metricized performance, you strip away a generation's primary coping mechanism and replace it with a continuous source of psychological dread.

This dread is compounded by the Comparison Trap we explored in earlier chapters, which hits the teenage brain with the force of a wrecking ball.

Adolescents are naturally insecure as they attempt to forge their identities. When you force a biologically insecure teenager to spend six hours a day looking at algorithmically perfected, beauty-filtered avatars of their peers, living highly curated, seemingly flawless lives, their self-esteem does not just drop; it shatters. They develop a persistent, agonizing internal monologue that tells them they are fundamentally broken, profoundly ugly, and entirely alone in their suffering.

The most damning aspect of this generational crisis is that it was not a blind spot for the Dopamine Cartel. Internal corporate leaks and whistleblower testimonies have repeatedly proven that the architects of the Matrix knew exactly what their products were doing. Their own proprietary research teams conducted massive studies detailing how their platforms directly exacerbated body dysmorphia in teenage girls and amplified suicidal ideation among vulnerable youth. They had the data in their hands. They saw the psychological carnage.

Yet, when faced with the choice between protecting a generation of children or maintaining the astronomical engagement metrics demanded by their shareholders, they chose the metrics. They buried the research. They tweaked the algorithms to push even more extreme, triggering content into the feeds of teenagers, because a teenager trapped in an anxious, obsessive loop is a highly profitable demographic.

We are watching a generation crumble under the weight of a virtual world they were never neurologically equipped to carry. They are drowning in a sea of artificial scarcity, curated perfection, and digital cruelty, all while the platforms extract billions of dollars from their deteriorating mental health.

The youth are the primary casualties of the Cartel's greed. But they are not the only ones being harvested. The Matrix demands raw material from every user, regardless of age, and it extracts this material with an invisible, terrifying efficiency. As we turn away from the psychological devastation of the youth and step into Chapter 8, we must confront the ultimate currency of the digital realm. We must examine the invisible commodity that makes the entire cartel possible: your data.

Chapter 8: Data: The Invisible Commodity

The previous chapters exposed how the Dopamine Cartel manipulates our emotions, weaponizes our insecurities, and dismantles our cognitive focus to keep us tethered to the screen. But human attention and emotional engagement are merely the extraction methods; they are not the final product. To understand the true, staggering scale of the digital empire, we must examine the raw material they are silently mining while we are distracted by curated outrage and impossible beauty standards.

Welcome to Chapter 8: Data: The Invisible Commodity.

The digital ecosystem is universally presented to the public as a suite of "free" services. You do not pay a monthly subscription to access a global search engine, create a social media profile, or use a highly accurate GPS navigation app. However, the foundational law of the modern digital economy dictates a grim, unavoidable reality: if you are not paying for the product, you are the product.

We begin this chapter by defining the economic engine driving this system in **Surveillance Capitalism Explained**. This is an entirely unprecedented mutation of global capitalism. Instead of extracting natural resources from the earth, this system claims private human experience as free raw material for hidden commercial practices of extraction, prediction, and sales. We will pull back the curtain on how the Matrix actually functions in the shadows. Every single digital interaction you make—every paused video, every deleted keystroke, every location ping, every heart rate measurement from a smartwatch, and every lingering glance on a screen—is meticulously harvested, aggregated, and fed into colossal, unregulated server farms to construct a hyper-accurate, ever-evolving digital twin of your life.

Next, we will explore exactly how this harvested raw material is monetized and weaponized in **Micro-Targeting and Behavioral Prediction**. The Cartel does not simply want to catalog what you purchased yesterday; they want to mathematically guarantee what you will do, feel, and believe tomorrow. We will examine how advanced artificial intelligence processes your massive digital footprint to map your deepest psychological vulnerabilities, your shifting political leanings, and your subconscious desires. By auctioning access to this predictive architecture, platforms allow advertisers, political campaigns, and unseen data brokers to serve you bespoke, highly calibrated stimuli. The goal is to bypass your rational defenses and manipulate your real-world behavior before you even realize a choice has been made for you.

Finally, we must confront the deeply unsettling reality of our environment in **The Illusion of Privacy in a Hyper-Connected World**. Millions of users still cling to outdated, analog notions of digital privacy, falsely believing that using complex passwords, browsing in incognito mode, clicking "accept" on terms of service, or toggling account settings affords them meaningful anonymity. We will dismantle this comforting fiction. In a modern ecosystem where smart appliances, vehicle telemetry, wearable technology, and ubiquitous background tracking are structurally required to participate in modern society, the concept of truly "opting out" has been structurally eradicated. We will examine how the very definition of privacy has been legally and deliberately eroded, transforming our private homes and our innermost thoughts into permanent, highly profitable surveillance zones.

By the end of this chapter, the invisible machinery of the digital economy will be laid bare. You will understand that every ounce of friction and anxiety you experience online is manufactured for a single, chilling purpose: to extract the blueprint of your mind and sell it on the open market.

8.1 Surveillance Capitalism Explained

For the first decade of the internet, the public operated under a dangerous, utopian delusion. We believed we were the beneficiaries of a miraculous new economy where global communication, infinite encyclopedias, and real-time navigation were provided entirely for free. We thought we were the consumers. We were wrong. The foundational law of the digital economy dictates that if a product is free, you are not the customer; you are the product. But even this popular cliché falls tragically short of the reality. You are not the product. Your private human experience is the unpriced raw material.

To understand the architecture of the Matrix, we must understand the economic engine that powers it: Surveillance Capitalism.

Traditional capitalism relied on extracting natural resources—timber, oil, land—and refining them into valuable commodities to be sold. Surveillance capitalism operates on the exact same extractive logic, but it claims a new, entirely unregulated, and infinitely renewable frontier: human life itself. The engineers of the Dopamine Cartel realized early on that every single human interaction within a digital space generates data. Initially, this "data exhaust" was simply used to improve the services themselves, making search engines more accurate or feeds load faster. But a profound, irreversible shift occurred when the Cartel realized that this collateral data was vastly more valuable than the services they were providing.

When we think of corporate data collection, we usually imagine a sterile digital filing cabinet containing our name, age, gender, and search history. This is an outdated, analog view of a highly advanced predatory system. The Cartel is not merely collecting demographic facts; they are harvesting behavioral surplus. They track how long your thumb hovers over a specific image before you scroll away. They record the exact geographic coordinates of your device every second of the day, mapping your daily commute, the doctors you visit, and the businesses you frequent. They monitor the cadence of your typing and the pressure of your keystrokes to detect micro-fluctuations in your emotional state, determining if you are tired, anxious, or angry. Every heartbeat recorded by a smartwatch, every seemingly private question asked to a smart speaker, and every micro-hesitation on a screen is silently vacuumed up into colossal, proprietary server farms.

Inside these massive computational centers, this incomprehensible volume of raw, behavioral data is fed into advanced artificial intelligence algorithms. The machine's singular goal is to process this raw material to construct a hyper-accurate, continuously updating "digital twin" of your mind.

This digital twin is a masterpiece of corporate surveillance. It knows more about your psychological vulnerabilities, your shifting political leanings, your sexual preferences, and your subconscious desires than your closest friends, your spouse, or even you do. It maps your emotional triggers and your deepest aspirations with cold, mathematical precision. It knows what time of day your willpower is lowest. It knows what specific shade of political rhetoric will cause your heart rate to spike.

But what does the Cartel do with these digital twins? Contrary to popular belief, they do not simply sell your personal data directly to third parties—doing so would surrender their ultimate monopoly. Instead, they sell *predictions*.

Surveillance capitalism operates as a massive, invisible marketplace where the primary commodities being traded are human behavioral futures. Just as Wall Street traders bet on pork bellies or oil futures, the Cartel auctions off the guaranteed ability to predict and influence what you will do, what you will buy, and how you will vote. They sell absolute, mathematical certainty to advertisers, political campaigns, and unseen data brokers.

This is where passive extraction evolves into active manipulation. Once the algorithm successfully maps your behavior, it seamlessly moves to modify it. Because the Cartel controls the digital environment you inhabit, they can subtly alter the parameters of your reality to guarantee the specific outcome their clients paid for. They know precisely which emotional trigger—be it a spark of outrage, a pang of insecurity, or a flash of validation—will reliably push you to click a link, purchase a supplement, or change your stance on a social issue. We have transitioned from an era of mass surveillance into a terrifying era of mass behavioral modification at scale.

This entire ecosystem relies on profound, structural asymmetry. The Cartel knows absolutely everything about us, while their operations remain locked behind impenetrable walls of corporate secrecy, trade protections, and proprietary black-box algorithms. We surrender the most intimate details of our inner lives in exchange for the convenience of instant communication and social validation, blindly signing incomprehensible Terms of Service agreements that act as legal shields for our own exploitation.

We have allowed the wealthiest corporations in human history to claim our thoughts, our movements, and our emotions as free, unclaimed territory for commercial extraction. We are the first generation to be mined not for the labor of our bodies, but for the predictable reactions of our neurology. And as the technology driving this extraction grows exponentially more sophisticated, it is moving far beyond basic advertising into the realm of absolute psychological control.

8.2 Micro-Targeting and Behavioral Prediction

In the physical world, traditional advertising is a blunt instrument. A billboard on a crowded highway or a commercial broadcast during a sporting event operates on the law of averages. The advertiser pays a massive premium to shout their message to millions of people, hoping that a tiny fraction of that audience happens to be interested, receptive, and in the mood to purchase. Surveillance capitalism, however, views the law of averages as an archaic inefficiency. The raw, behavioral data harvested in the previous section is useless until it is refined and weaponized. This weaponization is known as micro-targeting, and it represents a terrifying paradigm shift in the science of human persuasion.

o grasp the true power of micro-targeting, we must understand the transition from basic demographics to deep psychographics. Historically, marketers grouped people by broad, superficial categories: women aged eighteen to thirty-five, or high-income earners living in specific postal codes. The Dopamine Cartel operates on a much deeper, neurological level. Through the billions of seemingly innocuous data points you generate daily—the specific aesthetic of the photos you linger on, the cadence and speed of your scrolling, the vocabulary you utilize in private messages, and the precise times of day you are most active—the algorithm constructs a hyper-specific psychographic profile.

It maps your mind based on established psychological models, such as the Big Five personality traits: openness, conscientiousness, extroversion, agreeableness, and neuroticism. The machine deduces your personality with a level of accuracy that often surpasses human intuition. It knows if you are highly neurotic, making you uniquely susceptible to fear-based messaging. It knows if you are highly agreeable, making you prone to peer pressure and social conformity. The Cartel does not simply know what you buy; they know exactly *why* you buy it, what you deeply fear, and what specific emotional levers will reliably bypass your rational defenses.

Once this psychographic blueprint is established, the system moves from analysis to its ultimate objective: behavioral prediction. This is the holy grail of the Attention Economy. Utilizing massive server farms and advanced predictive artificial intelligence, the Cartel runs endless simulations based on your digital twin. It calculates the statistical probability of your future actions. The algorithm can predict when a user is likely to end a romantic relationship, when they are entering a depressive episode, when they are pregnant before they have told their family, or when they are most susceptible to a radical political ideology.

This predictive architecture is then placed on the open market in a continuous, real-time, automated auction. When you open a social media application, it takes mere milliseconds for the feed to load. In that microscopic sliver of time, an invisible bidding war occurs. But the buyers—multinational corporations, obscure data brokers, and shadowy political action committees—are not bidding for banner space. They are bidding for guaranteed access to your current emotional state. They are purchasing the algorithmic certainty that if they show you a specific image, paired with a customized headline, at the exact moment your willpower is mathematically calculated to be at its lowest, you will perform the desired action.

Consider the sheer asymmetry of this encounter. You might be sitting on your couch, exhausted after a long day, casually swiping through your phone. You are in a passive, unguarded, and vulnerable state. Yet, on the other side of the glass, an invisible supercomputer has just determined that your recent digital behavior indicates a temporary spike in health anxiety and a drop in self-esteem. In real-time, it auctions this specific vulnerability to a wellness company. The company deploys an advertisement explicitly designed to trigger that exact anxiety, utilizing colors, fonts, and language mathematically optimized to defeat your specific psychological defenses. You click "buy," falsely believing you made a conscious, independent choice to improve your life, entirely unaware that the transaction was mathematically guaranteed before you even saw the product.

This is not marketing; it is behavioral engineering at scale. And its applications extend far beyond commerce. The exact same infrastructure used to sell you a pair of running shoes is utilized to sell you a political reality. Over the last decade, political operatives have leveraged micro-targeting to devastating effect. They do not need to persuade the masses with broad policy arguments; they only need to manipulate the margins. By exploiting the psychographic vulnerabilities of a few thousand key individuals in swing districts—injecting highly customized, inflammatory outrage directly into the feeds of those mathematically predicted to be susceptible to it—they can alter the trajectory of democratic elections.

The most insidious aspect of behavioral prediction is that it eventually ceases to be a mere prediction. Once the Matrix knows exactly how you will react to a specific stimulus, it begins to actively shape your digital environment to ensure that reaction occurs. It curates your reality to guarantee the outcome its clients paid for. We are being steered through our lives by invisible algorithmic nudges, making choices we fiercely believe are our own, entirely blind to the digital strings attached to our prefrontal cortex.

This level of total, intimate control is only possible because we have voluntarily surrendered the boundaries of our private lives. But as we will explore in the final section of this chapter, the Cartel did not just ask for our privacy; they structurally eradicated the very concept of it.

8.3 The Illusion of Privacy in a Hyper-Connected World

Despite the overwhelming evidence of mass data extraction and algorithmic micro-targeting, millions of users still cling to a comforting, deeply outdated fiction. We desperately convince ourselves that we still possess agency over our digital lives. We believe that by using complex passwords, periodically clearing our browser history, utilizing "incognito" modes, or manually toggling our location services off, we are successfully maintaining a defensive perimeter around our private worlds. We are suffering from an analog hangover—applying twentieth-century concepts of privacy to a twenty-first-century ubiquitous surveillance grid. The Dopamine Cartel actively encourages this delusion because as long as you believe privacy is merely a setting you can control, you will not question the structural reality that true privacy has been systematically eradicated.

The foundational pillar of this illusion is the weaponization of consent. Whenever we download a new application, create an account, or update an operating system, we are presented with a labyrinthine Terms of Service agreement. We click "Accept" in a fraction of a second. The legal framework of the modern internet relies heavily on this single click to claim that we have willfully consented to our own surveillance. But this is the greatest legal fiction of our era. These agreements are not good-faith contracts between equal parties; they are digital ultimatums. They are written in impenetrable legalese, designed specifically to be unreadable and exhausting for the average consumer.

More importantly, consent cannot mathematically exist when the alternative to agreement is exile from modern society. If you refuse the terms of service for a major tech conglomerate, you are not simply opting out of a trivial social network; you are severing your ability to communicate with your child's school, navigate a metropolitan city, apply for corporate employment, or access digital banking. The Cartel has woven its proprietary tracking infrastructure so deeply into the fundamental fabric of daily human functioning that participation is essentially mandatory. To say a user "consents" to data extraction under these conditions is akin to saying a drowning person "consents" to handing over their wallet in exchange for a life preserver. It is extortion cleverly disguised as a user agreement.

Even if an individual attempts the herculean, isolating task of living entirely off the digital grid, the Matrix still manages to map their existence through "shadow profiling." The Cartel's tracking infrastructure—invisible pixels, embedded social plug-ins, and third-party cookies—is injected into the code of virtually every website and digital service on earth. You do not need to possess an account on a major platform for that platform to build a comprehensive, highly accurate dossier on you. They track your IP address as you browse the web, they scrape your phone number from the contact lists of friends and family who *did* download their apps, and they triangulate your physical location based on the public Wi-Fi networks your phone passively pings as you walk down the street. In the hyper-connected world, you are surveilled by association.

Furthermore, the surveillance has seamlessly breached the final physical sanctuary of human existence: the home. We no longer just carry the Matrix in our pockets; we have actively, voluntarily installed it in our living rooms, our kitchens, and our bedrooms under the guise of the "Internet of Things" (IoT). The corporate push to make every household appliance "smart" was never truly about user convenience; it was about closing the data loop.

A smart thermostat does not merely regulate temperature; it maps the exact hours you are awake, asleep, and away from the house. An internet-connected television monitors not just what you watch, but tracks the micro-movements of your remote to gauge your engagement levels during commercials. Voice-activated virtual assistants condition us to speak our private queries out loud in our own homes, normalizing the presence of a permanently open corporate microphone sitting on the kitchen counter. We willingly paid hundreds of dollars for the hardware required to wiretap our own houses, seduced by the trivial convenience of adjusting the lighting with a voice command or checking a digital doorbell from across the globe.

The psychological toll of living within this hyper-connected panopticon is subtle, invisible, but profoundly damaging. In the late eighteenth century, philosopher Jeremy Bentham designed a theoretical prison called the Panopticon. The genius of the design was that the inmates could never tell exactly when the guard was watching them, meaning they had to assume they were being watched at all times. Consequently, they began to strictly police their own behavior. The Cartel has constructed a digital Panopticon on a planetary scale.

When we subconsciously internalize that every search query is logged, every private message is scanned, and every physical movement is tracked, a chilling effect washes over our behavior. We begin to self-censor. We hesitate before searching for a controversial medical symptom, exploring a radical political philosophy, or viewing a piece of fringe art, terrified of how that query might permanently alter our algorithmic profile or be weaponized against us by an unseen data broker in the future. The illusion of privacy forces us to perform a sanitized, socially acceptable version of ourselves even when we are completely alone in an empty room.

True individuality, deep intellectual exploration, and meaningful societal progress have historically required the safety of the shadows—private spaces where radical ideas can be tested, mistakes can be made, and unpopular thoughts can be explored without immediate public consequence. By eradicating the shadows and illuminating every corner of human existence with the sterile, unforgiving light of data extraction, the Matrix does not just track who we are; it actively limits who we are willing to become.

Chapter 9: The Physical Toll of the Matrix

The narrative of the digital age often treats the human body as an irrelevant relic—a clumsy, analog vessel whose only remaining purpose is to transport a glowing screen from one room to another. We have spent the preceding chapters charting the devastating psychological, emotional, and societal damage inflicted by the Dopamine Cartel. We have examined how they map our minds, manipulate our insecurities, and harvest our data. But the Matrix does not merely exist in the ethereal realm of the cloud; it exerts a brutal, undeniable gravity on our physical flesh.

Welcome to Chapter 9: The Physical Toll of the Matrix.

While we obsess over the degradation of our attention spans and the fracturing of our political discourse, a silent, physiological crisis is unfolding. The human body is a masterpiece of biomechanical engineering, forged over millions of years of active, dynamic movement. It was not designed to be folded into a rigid, forward-leaning crescent, immobilized for twelve hours a day in a state of high-arousal stasis. In this chapter, we will ground the abstract threats of the digital world in the stark, biological realities of what the screen is actively doing to our anatomy.

We begin with the structural collapse of the human frame in **Tech Neck, Sedentary Habits, and Muscle Atrophy**. The posture we assume when engaging with our devices is not neutral; it is the biological posture of submission and depression. We will explore how hours of staring down at a phone effectively hangs a sixty-pound weight from the cervical spine, leading to a modern epidemic of chronic pain, spinal degeneration, and systemic muscle atrophy. The Matrix demands our absolute stillness, and our musculoskeletal system is paying a devastating price for that compliance.

Next, we will examine the theft of our most critical biological reset mechanism in **The Devastating Impact of Blue Light on Sleep Cycles**. Sleep is not merely a period of inactivity; it is the essential maintenance window for cellular repair, memory consolidation, and hormonal balance. We will break down the neuroscience of how the hyper-specific wavelength of light emitted by our screens effectively hacks the brain's ancient circadian rhythm, tricking the pineal gland into believing it is perpetually high noon. We will uncover how this engineered insomnia is driving a global surge in exhaustion, metabolic dysfunction, and weakened immune systems.

Finally, we will investigate the toxic chemical bath our devices force us to endure in **Cortisol and the Chronic Stress of Constant Notifications**. The human fight-or-flight response was designed to save us from apex predators, not to alert us to a new group chat message or a promotional email. We will look at how the unpredictable, intermittent vibrations and chimes of our devices keep the nervous system locked in a permanent state of low-grade panic, flooding the bloodstream with cortisol and adrenaline and accelerating cellular aging.

By the end of this chapter, the illusion of a harmless, disembodied digital life will be entirely shattered. You will understand that the Attention Economy is not just changing how you think; it is actively, structurally breaking down the body you inhabit.

9.1 Tech Neck, Sedentary Habits, and Muscle Atrophy

The human body is a testament to the evolutionary necessity of movement. For hundreds of thousands of years, our survival depended on our ability to run, climb, hunt, and forage. Our musculoskeletal system was meticulously engineered for dynamic, upright mobility. But the Dopamine Cartel has engineered an environment that demands the exact opposite. The Attention Economy cannot monetize a human being who is actively moving through the physical world. To extract your behavioral data and feed you targeted advertisements, the Matrix requires your absolute, unwavering stillness. The screen demands that you stop moving, sit down, and fold your body into a highly specific, biologically disastrous shape.

The most immediate and visible casualty of this forced stasis is the cervical spine, giving rise to a modern physiological epidemic clinically referred to as "Tech Neck." To understand the severity of this condition, we must look at the basic physics of the human skeleton. An average adult human head weighs approximately ten to twelve pounds when balanced perfectly upright, supported by a natural, slight curve in the neck. In this neutral position, the skeletal structure bears the load efficiently, requiring minimal muscular effort to remain balanced.

However, the digital interface fundamentally breaks this alignment. When you hold a smartphone in your hands and tilt your head downward to scroll, the laws of physics aggressively multiply the weight of your skull. At a mere fifteen-degree forward tilt, the force exerted on the cervical spine increases to twenty-seven pounds. At a forty-five-degree tilt, the weight surges to nearly fifty pounds. And at a sixty-degree angle—the standard, hunched posture of a user deeply engrossed in a social media feed—your neck is struggling to support sixty pounds of pressure. This is the physiological equivalent of hanging a heavy bowling ball from your neck for an average of five to seven hours every single day.

The biological hardware was simply not designed to withstand this sustained load. When forced into this unnatural position for thousands of hours a year, the muscles at the back of the neck and the shoulders are subjected to constant, agonizing tension as they fight to keep the head from falling entirely forward. Over time, the ligaments stretch and lose their necessary elasticity. The discs between the cervical vertebrae—the vital shock absorbers of the spine—are subjected to extreme, asymmetrical compression. This leads to premature disc degeneration, herniation, and nerve compression. Orthopedic surgeons are now routinely diagnosing young adults in their twenties with the severe spinal degradation and osteoarthritis previously reserved for the elderly. We are actively crushing our own spines to look at a glass rectangle.

But the physical toll of the Matrix extends far beyond the neck. The demand for constant screen engagement has normalized a state of hyper-sedentary existence. The modern chair has become the physical anchor of the digital cage. When you sit in a hunched position for hours on end, a cascade of physiological failures begins throughout the entire body. The hip flexors—the muscles connecting the torso to the legs—remain in a perpetually shortened and tightened state, pulling the pelvis out of alignment and triggering chronic lower back pain.

Simultaneously, the gluteal muscles, which are the largest and most powerful muscles in the human body, essentially go to sleep. Medical professionals refer to this as "gluteal amnesia." Because these muscles are not required to bear weight or stabilize the pelvis during prolonged sitting, the neuromuscular pathways that activate them begin to atrophy. We lose our foundational strength. We trade the robust, dynamic capability of the human frame for soft, weakened bodies incapable of basic athletic function.

Furthermore, the physical posture demanded by our devices—shoulders rolled forward, chest collapsed, head bowed—severely restricts our respiratory capacity. When the chest cavity is compressed, the diaphragm cannot fully expand. We are forced to take shallow, rapid breaths from the upper chest. This restricted breathing directly signals the autonomic nervous system that the body is in a state of distress, artificially elevating heart rates and triggering a low-grade physiological panic.

This reveals the most insidious aspect of the physical toll: the mind-body feedback loop. In the animal kingdom, and deep within human psychology, the physical posture of folding inward, rounding the shoulders, and bowing the head is the universal biological expression of submission, defeat, and depression. You cannot force your body into the posture of depression for eight hours a day without your brain eventually receiving the chemical signal that you are, in fact, depressed. The Matrix forces us into a literal slump, ensuring our physical posture perfectly mirrors the psychological anxiety it is actively manufacturing.

We are systematically dismantling the structural integrity of our bodies in exchange for digital connection. Yet, this muscular atrophy and skeletal deformation is only the first phase of the physical assault. As the sun sets and the physical body attempts to enter its necessary phase of biological repair, the screen deploys its next weapon, actively hijacking the deepest, most ancient rhythms of the human brain.

9.2 The Devastating Impact of Blue Light on Sleep Cycles

To fully grasp the physical damage inflicted by the Matrix, we must fundamentally change how we view sleep. In modern, hyper-productive society, sleep is often treated as a luxury, a biological inconvenience, or merely a passive state of doing nothing. This is a fatal misunderstanding of human physiology. Sleep is an intensely active, highly complex biological process. It is the critical maintenance window during which the brain clears out toxic metabolic byproducts, consolidates memories, repairs damaged cellular tissue, and recalibrates the immune system. Without deep, restorative sleep, the human body rapidly begins to break down.

For millions of years, the initiation of this vital repair cycle was governed by a single, infallible environmental cue: the sun.

Human biology operates on a circadian rhythm, a roughly twenty-four-hour internal clock orchestrated by a tiny region in the brain called the suprachiasmatic nucleus (SCN). The SCN is directly connected to the optic nerve. When the sun rises, it emits a broad spectrum of light, heavily concentrated in short, high-energy blue wavelengths. The photoreceptors in our eyes detect this blue light, signaling the SCN to suppress sleep hormones and flood the body with cortisol, waking us up and preparing us for the day. As the sun sets and the sky turns into warmer, low-energy hues of red and orange, the lack of blue light signals the SCN to activate the pineal gland. The pineal gland then releases melatonin, the hormone that lowers our core body temperature, slows our heart rate, and pulls us into deep, restorative sleep.

This elegant, ancient biological system worked flawlessly for the entirety of human evolution. Then, the tech industry introduced the Light Emitting Diode (LED) screen, and completely hacked the human circadian rhythm.

The screens on our smartphones, tablets, and laptops do not emit a neutral, natural light. They are specifically engineered to emit a massive, concentrated blast of high-energy artificial blue light. The physics of this light perfectly mimic the exact wavelength of the midday sun.

When you lie in bed at eleven o'clock at night, scrolling through a social media feed or watching a video, you are blinding your optic nerve with a synthetic noon. Your biological hardware cannot distinguish between the sun in the sky and the glowing rectangle in your hand. The SCN detects the blue light and instantly sends a panic signal to the pineal gland, halting the production of melatonin entirely. You are forcing your brain to chemically believe it is the middle of the day, effectively orchestrating your own insomnia.

The consequences of this biochemical deception are catastrophic. Even if you eventually manage to fall asleep after putting the device away, the residual suppression of melatonin severely degrades the architecture of your sleep. You spend more time in light, fragmented sleep stages and are robbed of the deep, slow-wave sleep required for physical restoration, and the REM (Rapid Eye Movement) sleep required for emotional regulation.

When we systematically deprive the body of this maintenance window, the physiological fallout is systemic. Medical science has drawn a direct, undeniable line between chronic, screen-induced sleep deprivation and severe metabolic dysfunction. A lack of deep sleep disrupts the delicate balance of ghrelin and leptin—the hormones that regulate hunger and satiety—causing intense cravings for high-calorie, sugary foods and directly contributing to the global obesity epidemic. It suppresses the immune system, making the body exponentially more vulnerable to infection. It elevates baseline blood pressure and dramatically increases the long-term risk of cardiovascular disease.

Most terrifyingly, it prevents the brain's glymphatic system from flushing out amyloid-beta, a toxic protein plaque that accumulates during waking hours. The chronic buildup of this specific plaque is one of the primary biological markers for Alzheimer's disease and severe cognitive decline. We are not just making ourselves tired; we are actively accelerating the aging of our own neurological hardware.

The Dopamine Cartel is fully aware of the biology of blue light. The integration of "night mode" or "blue light filters" on modern devices is a quiet, legal admission of guilt—a performative band-aid placed over a gaping biological wound. They know the screen damages your sleep, but they have absolutely no financial incentive to actually let you rest.

In the Attention Economy, a sleeping user is an unprofitable user. Sleep is the only period of the day when you are not generating behavioral data, viewing advertisements, or feeding the algorithm. The Cartel views your biological need for rest not as a boundary to be respected, but as a competitor to be defeated. By combining the psychological trap of the infinite scroll with the physiological hack of artificial blue light, they have successfully conquered the night, extracting billions of dollars in revenue from the hours you were supposed to spend healing.

We drag our exhausted, malnourished bodies out of bed the next morning, artificially jumpstarting our systems with caffeine to survive another day in the Matrix. But the blue light is only the setup. As we will see in the next section, once the Cartel has successfully disrupted our rest, they deploy an endless stream of digital threats to keep our nervous systems locked in a state of permanent, toxic stress.

9.3 Cortisol and the Chronic Stress of Constant Notifications

The human nervous system is an ancient, highly tuned survival instrument. For the vast majority of our evolutionary history, the environment was fraught with immediate, physical dangers. To survive, our bodies developed a sophisticated alarm network: the autonomic nervous system. When our prehistoric ancestors heard a sudden, unpredictable noise—a snapping twig or a rustling in the tall grass—the brain's threat-detection center, the amygdala, fired instantaneously. This triggered the sympathetic nervous system to initiate a "fight-or-flight" response. In a fraction of a second, the adrenal glands flooded the bloodstream with adrenaline and cortisol. The heart rate spiked, blood pressure surged, pupils dilated, and the digestive and immune systems were temporarily shut down to reroute all available metabolic energy to the muscles.

This biochemical cascade is a physiological masterpiece designed to give a human being the explosive strength and hyper-focus necessary to sprint away from a predator or engage in physical combat. But crucially, this extreme state of biological arousal was designed to be rare, and it was designed to be brief. Once the threat passed, the parasympathetic nervous system—the "rest and digest" network—would step in, clear the toxic stress hormones from the bloodstream, and return the body to a calm, restorative baseline.

The engineers of the Dopamine Cartel have effectively weaponized this ancient survival mechanism. They recognized that the most efficient way to capture human attention is to bypass the rational prefrontal cortex and directly trigger the amygdala.

When your smartphone violently vibrates in your pocket, or emits a sudden, piercing chime to announce a new email, a direct message, or a breaking news alert, your conscious mind might know that you are perfectly safe sitting at your desk. But your limbic system does not know what an email is. To the primitive architecture of your brain, a sudden, unpredictable acoustic or tactile interruption is perceived as an environmental anomaly. It is the digital equivalent of a snapping twig in the dark.

Every single notification triggers a micro-dose of the fight-or-flight response. The amygdala fires. A subtle wave of adrenaline and cortisol enters the bloodstream. Your heart rate slightly elevates, your breathing becomes shallower, and your muscles microscopically tense. If this happened once or twice a week, the body could easily manage the recovery. But the Matrix operates on a scale of relentless bombardment.

The average digital consumer receives dozens, if not hundreds, of push notifications, alerts, and digital interruptions every single day.

Because the threats are constant, the parasympathetic nervous system is never allowed to fully engage and clear the system. We are trapped in a state of permanent, low-grade biological panic. We are marinating our internal organs in a toxic, unending bath of stress hormones.

Medical science has meticulously documented the devastating physiological consequences of chronic cortisol exposure. Cortisol is highly corrosive when left in the bloodstream for extended periods. It actively suppresses the immune system, leaving the body exponentially more vulnerable to viral and bacterial infections. It induces widespread, systemic inflammation, which is now recognized as the biological root of nearly every modern chronic disease. It disrupts the endocrine system, leading to insulin resistance, stubborn weight gain around the midsection, and severe digestive disorders like Irritable Bowel Syndrome.

Furthermore, chronic exposure to stress hormones causes literal, structural damage to the cardiovascular system. The constant, artificial elevation of blood pressure acts like sandpaper on the inner lining of the arteries, accelerating the buildup of plaque and dramatically increasing the risk of hypertension, heart attacks, and strokes. By subjecting ourselves to the endless, unpredictable rhythm of digital notifications, we are not just distracting ourselves; we are actively grinding down our biological hardware.

The psychological toll of this physical state is equally catastrophic. The Matrix employs a psychological principle known as "variable interval reinforcement." You never know exactly when a notification will arrive, nor do you know what it contains. It could be a text from a loved one, a promotion, a devastating piece of global news, or an angry email from a boss. This unpredictability creates a state of chronic hyper-vigilance. The nervous system is forced to remain constantly "on edge," waiting for the next strike. This is the physiological root of modern burnout. We are exhausted not because we are working too hard, but because our bodies are dedicating massive amounts of invisible metabolic energy just to brace for the next digital interruption.

Ultimately, the physical toll of the Matrix—the structural deformation of Tech Neck, the metabolic sabotage of blue-light insomnia, and the cardiovascular strain of chronic cortisol—reveals a dark, undeniable truth. The digital world is not a separate, ethereal reality that exists only in the cloud. It is a parasitic architecture that extracts its profits directly from our flesh, our bones, and our blood. We are sacrificing our physical vitality to sustain a machine that will never be satisfied.

Yet, recognizing the trap is only the first step. As we close the door on the diagnostic phases of this book and move toward the conclusion, we must pivot from understanding our subjugation to engineering our escape. We must outline the path forward.

Chapter 10: Recognizing Your Place in the Matrix

The preceding chapters have mapped the sprawling, predatory architecture of the Dopamine Cartel. We have examined how the Matrix manipulates our neurology, weaponizes our deepest insecurities, harvests our private data, and inflicts profound structural damage on our physical bodies. Up to this point, our exploration has been largely systemic. We have looked at the machine from the outside. But diagnosis without personal application is merely theory. To truly break free from the Attention Economy, you must move beyond a general understanding of how the algorithm exploits humanity and confront the uncomfortable reality of how it has successfully exploited *you*.

Welcome to Chapter 10: Recognizing Your Place in the Matrix.

This chapter marks the crucial pivot from passive observation to active reclamation. The journey toward cognitive autonomy begins with a ruthless, unfiltered assessment of your current reality. We will start this process by **Conducting an Honest Audit of Your Digital Diet**. For years, you have likely relied on the Cartel's most effective psychological shield: cognitive dissonance. We drastically underestimate our screen time, convincing ourselves that we only check our phones for a few minutes a day, while our devices quietly log thousands of hours of mindless consumption. We will strip away this self-deception, providing you with the framework to mathematically quantify your exact level of subjugation. You cannot dismantle a prison whose walls you refuse to measure.

Once we have established the raw numbers, we will move past the *how much* and interrogate the *why* by **Identifying Your Personal Algorithmic Triggers**. The Matrix does not use a universal lock to keep you trapped; it uses a bespoke, algorithmic key cut perfectly to the shape of your unique psychological vulnerabilities. We will guide you through the process of mapping your own internal landscape to discover what specific emotional states—be it chronic boredom, social anxiety, professional imposter syndrome, or profound loneliness—the algorithm is actively exploiting. The machine already knows exactly what drives you to pick up the glass rectangle. It is time you finally learned it for yourself.

Finally, we will navigate the complex reality of modern existence by **Defining the Line Between Utility and Abuse**. Escaping the Matrix does not require retreating to a cabin in the woods and severing all ties with modern technology. The internet remains a miraculous tool for genuine connection, professional advancement, and education. The goal is not eradication; the goal is subordination. We will establish clear, actionable parameters to help you identify the exact moment a digital platform ceases to function as a tool you wield, and becomes a master that wields you.

By the end of this chapter, the fog of algorithmic conditioning will lift. You will possess a stark, undeniable blueprint of your personal digital captivity, arming you with the critical self-awareness required to finally take the weapon out of the Cartel's hands.

10.1 Conducting an Honest Audit of Your Digital Diet

The human mind possesses a remarkable, deeply ingrained defense mechanism known as cognitive dissonance. When our actual behavior contradicts our fundamental belief about who we are, the brain actively alters our perception of reality to resolve the psychological friction. In the context of the Attention Economy, cognitive dissonance is the Dopamine Cartel's most effective shield. We all want to believe we are autonomous, rational individuals who use technology merely as a tool. Therefore, when we instinctively reach for our phones in the middle of a conversation, or lose three hours to an infinite scroll on a Tuesday night, our brains immediately generate a comforting rationalization. We tell ourselves we were just "checking a quick email," "unwinding for a few minutes," or "staying informed."

To break free from the Matrix, you must first brutally shatter this cognitive dissonance. You cannot defeat an adversary whose presence you refuse to acknowledge, and you cannot reclaim your time until you mathematically quantify exactly how much of it is being stolen. This requires conducting a relentless, strictly honest audit of your digital diet.

The first phase of this audit is purely quantitative, and ironically, the tools required to conduct it are built directly into the very devices that trap us. Every modern smartphone operating system features a screen time or digital wellbeing tracker. For the vast majority of users, these metrics are buried in the settings menu, deliberately ignored because the raw data they contain is profoundly uncomfortable to look at. Your first actionable step is to pull this data to the forefront.

Do not merely glance at your daily average of total hours spent on the screen. While seeing a number like "five hours and forty minutes" can be a necessary shock to the system, total time is only a surface-level metric. You must dig deeper into the behavioral analytics, specifically focusing on a metric often labeled as "pickups" or "unlocks."

The "pickups" metric records exactly how many times a day you sever your connection with physical reality to check the digital realm. It is common for an average user to unlock their phone between eighty to one hundred and fifty times a day. Let that number sink in. If you are awake for sixteen hours, a hundred pickups means you are fracturing your attention and triggering a context switch every nine minutes, all day, every day. This metric strips away the illusion that you are sitting down for dedicated, intentional sessions of digital use. It reveals the grim reality of chronic, compulsive checking. Furthermore, look at the "first used after waking" metric. If your device is unlocked within three minutes of your eyes opening, the Matrix has successfully colonized your morning, setting a reactive, highly anxious baseline for your entire day.

Once the objective, quantitative data has been established, you must move to the second, far more difficult phase: the qualitative audit.

Numbers reveal the scale of the extraction, but they do not reveal the emotional mechanics driving it. For this, you must temporarily rely on an analog tool. For three consecutive days, carry a small physical notebook and a pen. Every single time you feel the impulse to unlock your phone, before you actually touch the screen, you must write down three things.

First, note the physical environment. Where are you? Are you sitting at a red light, lying in bed, sitting on the toilet, or standing in an elevator? Mapping these locations reveals the physical spaces the Cartel has successfully infiltrated to eradicate your moments of quiet reflection.

Second, note the emotional trigger. What exactly were you feeling in the ten seconds before the urge to reach for the device hit you? Were you feeling a pang of imposter syndrome while struggling with a work task? Were you feeling a sudden wave of social isolation? Or were you simply experiencing the profound, agonizing boredom of waiting in a line?

Finally, after you finish your digital session and put the phone down, note your emotional state upon returning to reality. Do you feel genuinely rested, informed, and connected? Or do you feel a lingering sense of generalized anxiety, a sudden dissatisfaction with your own life, and a distinct lack of physical energy?

When you review this physical ledger at the end of the three days, the results are almost always universally devastating. The qualitative audit exposes the central lie of the digital ecosystem. You will clearly see that you are rarely opening these applications with intentionality or purpose. Instead, you are using the glass rectangle as a digital pacifier, a subconscious reflex designed to instantly numb any fleeting moment of emotional discomfort, boredom, or psychological friction.

Conducting this honest audit is an inherently painful process. It is designed to induce a profound sense of shock and, inevitably, a degree of shame. When you look at the raw data and realize you are voluntarily surrendering weeks of your conscious life every year to watch curated strangers perform algorithmic trends, the ego rebels. But this shock is entirely necessary. Normalizing this discomfort is the first step toward liberation. You are not witnessing a personal moral failure; you are looking at the highly predictable outcome of a trillion-dollar engineering effort designed to bypass your rational brain. By documenting the exact parameters of your captivity, you establish the baseline required for escape. You have mapped the symptoms. In the next section, we will use this data to diagnose the underlying disease.

10.2 Identifying Your Personal Algorithmic Triggers

The quantitative audit detailed in the previous section provided the raw mathematics of your captivity. It revealed the staggering frequency with which you abandon the physical world to enter the digital one. But numbers, no matter how shocking, only tell us *how often* the Matrix successfully initiates a capture. To truly dismantle the architecture of your subjugation, we must move from the quantitative to the psychological. We must interrogate the *why*.

The most terrifying achievement of the Dopamine Cartel is that it does not rely on a universal master key to keep humanity locked in the Attention Economy. Instead, the algorithm functions as a master locksmith, constantly observing, analyzing, and milling a bespoke digital key cut to the exact, unique shape of your individual psychological vulnerabilities. What keeps your neighbor endlessly scrolling will not necessarily work on you. The machine has mapped your specific emotional landscape, and to regain your cognitive autonomy, you must map it for yourself. You must identify your personal algorithmic triggers.

To do this, we must reframe how we view the physical act of picking up a smartphone. We are rarely making a conscious, rational choice to seek out specific information. Instead, the device functions as a digital pacifier for the adult mind. We instinctively reach for the glowing screen to self-medicate a moment of emotional friction. The trigger is the specific, uncomfortable emotion you experienced in the microscopic window of time—those crucial three to five seconds—right before you felt the overwhelming compulsion to unlock your device.

While the algorithm's profile of you is highly complex, the emotional vulnerabilities it exploits generally fall into a few primary categories. By examining the qualitative data you recorded in your physical ledger, you can begin to identify which of these invisible strings the Cartel is pulling most frequently.

The Void of Boredom

For many, the most pervasive trigger is the absolute inability to tolerate a lack of stimulation. For hundreds of thousands of years, boredom was a natural, biological resting state. It is the neurological void where creativity, introspection, and deep problem-solving take root. The Matrix has systematically rebranded this vital biological state as an intolerable agony. If your ledger reveals that you consistently unlock your phone while waiting in line, sitting at a red light, or during the three minutes your coffee is brewing, your primary trigger is the fear of your own unoccupied mind. The algorithm has successfully convinced your nervous system that silence is a threat.

Cognitive Friction and Professional Anxiety

This trigger operates primarily during periods of intended focus, perfectly undermining the deep work we explored in Chapter 6. You sit down to write a difficult report, analyze a complex spreadsheet, or study for a demanding exam. Inevitably, you hit a point of cognitive friction—the work becomes hard, and you experience a sudden spike of professional anxiety or imposter syndrome. Your brain immediately seeks an escape hatch. It wants a cheap, unearned victory. You reach for the phone to check your email or scroll a feed, artificially soothing your feeling of inadequacy with a micro-dose of dopamine. You are not actually seeking distraction; you are actively fleeing from the psychological discomfort of challenging work.

Social Isolation and the Illusion of Connection

Humans are biologically hardwired for tribal belonging. When we experience a pang of loneliness, our limbic system registers it as a survival threat. In the past, this uncomfortable feeling motivated us to reach out to a friend or engage with our physical community. Today, the Matrix intercepts that biological signal. If you find yourself mindlessly opening social media applications late at night, or immediately after a period of isolation, your trigger is the desperate need for connection. The algorithmic tragedy is that the Cartel feeds you a curated stream of parasocial interactions and other people's highlight reels, which only deepens your underlying sense of isolation and locks you into the Comparison Trap.

Existential Dread and the Outrage Loop

The final major trigger preys upon our evolutionary need for security. When the world feels chaotic, unpredictable, or dangerous, our natural instinct is to gather information to regain a sense of agency. The algorithm expertly detects this anxiety. If your ledger shows that you reach for your phone during moments of generalized stress, only to find yourself doomscrolling through apocalyptic news, political vitriol, or viral outrage, the machine has weaponized your fear. It feeds you a highly concentrated diet of threat-based content, keeping your cortisol levels spiked and ensuring you remain trapped in a state of high-arousal vigilance.

Identifying these triggers requires brutal self-honesty. You must look at the moments you reached for the screen and correctly name the underlying emotion. You must say to yourself, *"I am not checking the news right now; I am feeling overwhelmed by my current project."* Or, *"I am not opening Instagram to see what my friends are doing; I am feeling profoundly lonely."*

This process of identification is not an exercise in self-punishment; it is a tactical act of cognitive rebellion. When a psychological trigger operates in the dark, submerged in the subconscious limbic system, it possesses absolute power over your behavior. By observing the trigger and naming the emotion, you drag the impulse out of the shadows and force it into the rational, analytical prefrontal cortex. You strip the algorithm of its invisibility.

Once you know exactly which emotional levers the machine is attempting to pull, you can finally begin to build defenses against them. You can learn to sit with the boredom, push through the cognitive friction, or seek genuine human connection in the physical world. But true liberation also requires defining the boundaries of our digital engagement, which leads us to the final, necessary distinction in our escape plan: separating the indispensable utility of the internet from the engineered abuse of the Cartel.

10.3 Defining the Line Between Utility and Abuse

When confronted with the sheer scale of the Dopamine Cartel's manipulation, the most common knee-jerk reaction is a desire for total digital asceticism. We fantasize about throwing our smartphones into a river, deleting every account, and retreating to an analog life in the woods. But this reactionary fantasy is not only impractical; it fundamentally misunderstands the objective of our rebellion. The internet is arguably the greatest infrastructure of knowledge and connection ever engineered by human beings. It allows us to navigate unknown cities, instantly access the sum total of human information, and communicate across oceans. The goal of recognizing your place in the Matrix is not to destroy the technology; the goal is to ruthlessly subordinate it. To do this, we must clearly define the precise boundary between digital utility and digital abuse.

The line between utility and abuse hinges on a single, vital concept: the definition of a tool.

Consider a hammer sitting on a workbench in your garage. It is an incredibly effective tool. But the hammer is inert. It does not vibrate at two in the morning to demand that you come build a birdhouse. It does not track how long you look at it, nor does it attempt to manipulate your emotional state to ensure you never put it down. You approach the hammer with a specific, premeditated intention, you execute the physical task, and then you leave the hammer on the bench.

Digital utility perfectly mimics the behavior of the hammer. Applications like digital maps, mobile banking, weather forecasts, and direct messaging (when used to coordinate physical logistics) operate as inert tools. They solve a specific, real-world friction. You open them with intent, you retrieve the necessary information, and you immediately close them. When you are operating in the realm of utility, you are the master, and the device is the servant.

Digital abuse begins the exact millisecond the device ceases to be a tool and becomes an environment.

The Matrix was intentionally designed to blur this boundary. The Cartel knows that you will inevitably pick up your phone to utilize a valid tool—to check the weather or read an important email. Their objective is to hijack that moment of legitimate utility and convert it into a prolonged session of algorithmic consumption. You open your phone to check your bank balance, but a bright red notification badge catches your eye. You tap it, and suddenly you are pulled into a frictionless environment of infinite scrolling, targeted outrage, and social comparison. You intended to use the hammer, but you fell into the casino.

To enforce the line between utility and abuse, you must elevate the concept of intentionality to a rigid discipline. Intentionality acts as the psychological firewall against the Attention Economy. Before your finger ever touches the glass of your screen, you must be able to articulate a specific, executable goal. "I am opening this device to send a document to my colleague." "I am opening this device to check the route to the restaurant." If you cannot articulate a concrete objective—if you are reaching for the device simply because your hands are empty, because you feel a pang of anxiety, or because you are seeking a vague, undefined sense of entertainment—you are crossing the line into abuse. You are no longer using the machine; the machine is using you.

Establishing this line requires architectural changes to your digital landscape. You must actively decouple the tools from the traps. The most effective strategy is to strip your device's home screen of everything except pure utility. Your map, your calendar, your camera, and your ride-sharing apps can remain. But every single application designed to capture attention—social media platforms, endless news feeds, streaming services, and mobile games—must be removed, or at the very least, buried deep within a folder structure that requires deliberate effort to access. By forcing yourself to physically search for the traps, you introduce the necessary friction required for your prefrontal cortex to wake up, evaluate the impulse, and ask: "Is this utility, or is this abuse?"

Furthermore, defining this boundary requires abandoning the myth of "staying informed" or "staying connected" as valid excuses for endless consumption. Mindlessly consuming a curated, algorithmically hyper-charged feed of global misery is not staying informed; it is digital self-harm. Passively watching the filtered highlight reels of acquaintances is not staying connected; it is parasocial voyeurism. True connection and genuine information gathering are active, intentional pursuits, not passive states of algorithmic surrender.

You do not need to abandon the digital world to escape the Cartel. You simply need to demote it. By rigidly enforcing the boundary between utility and abuse, you strip the screen of its psychological power. It is no longer an oracle, a pacifier, or a master. It returns to being exactly what it was always meant to be: a piece of glass and metal in your pocket, completely powerless until you decide you have a specific use for it.

Having audited our behavior, identified our psychological triggers, and drawn the line between tool and trap, the diagnostic phase of our journey is complete. We know how the machine operates, and we know exactly how it has captured us. We are now ready to execute the final phase. We are ready to build the infrastructure of our permanent escape.

Chapter 11: The Digital Detox Protocol

In the previous chapter, we stripped away the comforting illusions of cognitive dissonance to confront the exact dimensions of your digital captivity. You have audited your screen time, identified the specific psychological triggers the algorithm exploits, and drawn a hard, uncompromising line between necessary digital utility and manufactured algorithmic abuse. Awareness, however, is not the same as freedom. Knowing that a trap exists does not automatically release you from its jaws. To truly sever the invisible tethers of the Attention Economy, you must move from passive realization to aggressive, structural action.

Welcome to Chapter 11: The Digital Detox Protocol.

This chapter is the tactical manual for your escape. It is not a collection of mild suggestions about "mindfulness" or "finding balance." The Dopamine Cartel does not negotiate with balance; it operates on a business model of total behavioral conquest. Therefore, your counter-offensive must be equally absolute. We will dismantle the digital architecture of your daily life and rebuild it with the explicit goal of protecting your cognitive autonomy.

We begin this protocol by actively sabotaging the Cartel's most effective weapon: convenience. In **Designing Environmental Frictions to Stop the Scroll**, we will explore how to re-engineer your physical and digital environments to make algorithmic consumption deliberately difficult. The Matrix relies on frictionless design to bypass your rational brain. By injecting hard, structural friction back into your devices—from grayscale screens and aggressive notification culls to physical lockboxes and password barriers—we will force your prefrontal cortex to wake up and intercept the impulse before the scroll can even begin.

Next, we will establish the physical and temporal borders of your new reality in **Setting Boundaries: Time-Blocking and Tech-Free Zones**. A mind without borders is territory ripe for colonization. We will guide you through the process of carving out non-negotiable sanctuaries in your daily schedule and physical home where the screen is strictly forbidden. You will learn to treat your attention as a finite, heavily guarded resource, utilizing ruthless time-blocking to protect your deep work and reclaiming spaces like the bedroom and the dinner table from digital intrusion.

Finally, we will address the psychological void left behind when you unplug the machine in **Replacing Virtual Hits with Real-World Fulfillment**. You cannot simply remove a deeply ingrained coping mechanism without providing a superior alternative. If you rip the digital pacifier away and replace it with nothing, you will inevitably relapse into the Matrix. We will outline strategies for systematically rebuilding an analog life rich in genuine friction, authentic human connection, and deep, tactile hobbies. You will learn to rewire your dopamine pathways, trading the cheap, fleeting chemical spikes of the feed for the profound, lasting satisfaction of the physical world.

By the end of this chapter, you will possess a rigid, actionable framework to detoxify your nervous system. You will no longer be a passive consumer wandering through a rigged casino; you will be the absolute architect of your own attention.

11.1 Designing Environmental Frictions to Stop the Scroll

To understand how to defeat the Dopamine Cartel, you must first understand their central design philosophy: the total eradication of friction. In the realm of user interface and user experience (UI/UX) design, "friction" refers to anything that slows down a user, requires them to make a conscious choice, or forces them to exert extra effort. For decades, the tech industry has spent billions of dollars engineering friction out of existence. Features like Face ID, biometric unlocks, infinite scrolling, pull-to-refresh, and auto-playing videos were not created for your convenience. They were engineered to make the transition from the physical world into the digital world as seamless and unconscious as possible. The goal is to ensure you are already ten posts deep into a feed before your rational brain even realizes you have picked up your phone.

Willpower is entirely useless against this architecture. Willpower is a finite cognitive resource that rapidly depletes throughout the day. If you rely on willpower to resist a frictionless trap, you will inevitably fail the moment you are tired, stressed, or emotionally compromised. The only way to win is to fundamentally change the architecture. You must become the engineer of your own digital environment by actively and aggressively reintroducing friction.

The first layer of this architectural rebellion occurs directly on the screen, targeting the visual triggers that initiate the dopamine loop. The most effective, immediate step you can take is to switch your device's display to grayscale. The Matrix operates like a digital casino, relying on hyper-stimulating, aggressively saturated colors—specifically the bright red of notification badges—to trigger a sense of urgency and reward in your limbic system. Grayscale instantly neuters this visual manipulation. When you strip away the color, the infinite scroll suddenly looks like a dull, monotonous spreadsheet. The visual spell is broken, and the brain rapidly loses interest.

The second layer of digital friction involves sabotaging the unlock sequence. The Cartel wants your phone to unlock the millisecond you look at it. You must revoke this privilege. Disable facial recognition and fingerprint scanning entirely. Replace them with a complex, alphanumeric password—something that requires at least fifteen characters and includes numbers and symbols. By forcing yourself to manually type a long, frustrating password every single time you want to access your device, you are injecting a crucial three-to-five-second delay into the process. This delay acts as a cognitive toll booth. It gives your prefrontal cortex just enough time to wake up, intercept the unconscious physical reflex, and ask: "Wait, do I actually need to look at this right now, or am I just bored?"

The third layer requires dismantling the home screen. The apps that steal the most of your time should never be visible when you unlock your phone. If you cannot bring yourself to permanently delete them, you must bury them. Remove them from the home screen and place them inside a folder, place that folder on the fourth page of your app library, and bury the specific app on the third page of that folder. Furthermore, log out of the application after every use, forcing yourself to enter your username and password the next time you want to engage. By piling on these micro-frictions, you transform algorithmic consumption from a passive, accidental stumble into a highly deliberate, annoying chore.

Once you have secured the digital architecture, you must move to the physical architecture of your environment. The proximity of the device dictates the probability of the distraction. If your smartphone is sitting face-up on your desk while you attempt to do deep work, your brain is actively dedicating background processing power to ignore it. The friction of picking it up is zero. You must implement the "arm's length rule." When you are working, conversing, or resting, the device must never be within physical reach. Place it in a drawer, on a high shelf across the room, or in a completely different part of the house. The simple physical requirement of having to stand up, walk across the room, and retrieve the device is often enough friction to prevent the scroll entirely.

For those who find the physical compulsion too strong to break through proximity alone, tactile frictions can be incredibly effective. A common technique is placing a thick, physical rubber band horizontally across the center of your phone screen. You can still answer calls and access basic utilities, but the rubber band makes scrolling physically awkward and visually obstructed. It introduces a bizarre, tactile anomaly into the smooth, glass experience. It feels wrong in your hand, and that feeling of "wrongness" jolts you out of the zombie-like trance of the scroll. In extreme cases, users can purchase timed lockboxes—originally designed for locking away junk food—to physically imprison their devices for set intervals.

The objective of designing environmental friction is not to punish yourself. It is to force a wedge of time and effort between the impulse to check your phone and the action of actually doing it. The Dopamine Cartel relies on your unconscious compliance. By littering your physical and digital environment with speed bumps, locked doors, and frustrating hurdles, you ensure that every interaction with the Matrix is a conscious, negotiated choice. You are no longer falling down the rabbit hole; you are demanding to see the map before you take a single step.

11.2 Setting Boundaries: Time-Blocking and Tech-Free Zones

A mind without borders is a territory primed for algorithmic colonization. For the Dopamine Cartel to maximize its extraction of your behavioral data, it must operate on a fundamental assumption of total, unrestricted access to your time and your physical space. They have intentionally dissolved the traditional boundaries that once separated work from rest, public life from private sanctuary, and urgent crisis from idle entertainment. To successfully detoxify your nervous system, you cannot simply rely on the environmental frictions we established in the previous section. You must aggressively reclaim your territory by drawing rigid, non-negotiable borders across both your daily schedule and your physical home.

We begin with the defense of your temporal borders through the discipline of time-blocking. The Matrix has conditioned us to live in a state of continuous partial attention. We keep our email clients open, our notifications buzzing, and our feeds refreshing while simultaneously attempting to execute complex tasks, converse with our families, or wind down for the night. This constant bleeding of digital demands into every margin of the day is exactly what drives the severe cognitive fatigue we explored in Chapter 6.

Time-blocking is the radical act of treating your attention as a finite, heavily guarded resource. Instead of allowing the digital world to interrupt you at will, you dictate exactly when the digital world is permitted to speak. This requires segmenting your day into strict, uncompromising intervals. When you enter a block dedicated to deep work, you sever the connection entirely—closing tabs, silencing devices, and utilizing website blockers.

But time-blocking also applies to consumption. You must schedule specific, contained windows for checking emails, responding to messages, and even engaging with social media if you have deemed it a necessary utility. By batch-processing these digital tasks into two or three dedicated thirty-minute windows a day, you force the chaotic stream of the Attention Economy into a predictable, manageable pipeline. You transition from a reactive victim of the algorithm to an intentional director of your own schedule.

However, temporal boundaries are virtually impossible to maintain if your physical environment remains entirely compromised. The smartphone is the first invention in human history that successfully collapsed all physical context. Historically, you went to an office to work, a theater to be entertained, and a home to rest. Today, the glass rectangle in your pocket contains your office, the global news cycle, the shopping mall, and the theater, effectively transforming every room you enter into a digital command center. To break this spatial collapse, you must establish strict Tech-Free Zones within your home.

The most critical battleground is the bedroom. As we detailed in Chapter 9, the Cartel actively weaponizes blue light and intermittent anxiety to destroy your sleep architecture. The bedroom must be reclaimed as an absolute sanctuary for biological rest and human intimacy. The smartphone cannot simply be placed face down on the nightstand; it must be banished from the room entirely. This requires a minor analog investment: purchase a basic digital or mechanical alarm clock. By removing the smartphone from the bedroom, you protect your vulnerable neurological state in the final moments before sleep, and you guarantee that your morning begins with your own autonomous thoughts, rather than the curated, panic-inducing agenda of a global feed.

The second mandatory Tech-Free Zone is the dining table. The dining room has served as the sacred anchor of human connection for millennia. Yet, it has become completely normalized to place a glowing device next to the dinner plate. Studies in behavioral psychology have demonstrated that the mere physical presence of a smartphone on a table, even if it is turned off, actively degrades the quality of conversation and reduces empathy between the people sitting there. The brain is subconsciously dedicating processing power to the possibility of an incoming interruption. By enforcing a strict ban on devices during meals, you force yourself to be entirely present, honoring the people sitting across from you and signaling to your nervous system that the immediate, physical world takes absolute precedence over the virtual one.

Finally, you must reclaim the micro-sanctuaries of solitude, such as the bathroom. The modern reflex to carry a device into the bathroom represents a total surrender of the day's final moments of quiet, unstructured thought. These brief pauses in stimulation are vital for the brain's default mode network to process ideas and regulate emotions. When we surrender them to the scroll, we systematically suffocate our own internal monologue.

Enforcing these temporal and physical boundaries will initially trigger a profound sense of psychological withdrawal. You will reach into an empty pocket; you will feel phantom vibrations; you will experience the sudden, sharp panic of being disconnected. This discomfort is the exact measure of your addiction leaving the body. But as you hold the line, the panic will inevitably subside, replaced by a deep, expansive silence. You will discover that by locking the Matrix out of specific hours and rooms, you have suddenly created a vast, open space in your life. The challenge, as we will explore in the final section of this protocol, is knowing exactly how to fill it.

11.3 Replacing Virtual Hits with Real-World Fulfillment

When you successfully implement environmental frictions and establish rigid digital boundaries, you will inevitably confront a terrifying reality: the void. For years, the Matrix has acted as an algorithmic intravenous drip, delivering a steady, predictable supply of cheap dopamine directly to your limbic system. When you suddenly sever that line, your brain does not immediately return to a state of calm, analog baseline. It panics. It experiences genuine, chemical withdrawal. You will find yourself standing in your living room, the evening stretching out before you, entirely unaccustomed to the sheer volume of silence. If you do not have a deliberate, aggressive strategy to fill this sudden expanse of time, the discomfort of the void will overpower your willpower, and you will inevitably relapse. You cannot simply remove a deeply ingrained coping mechanism; you must actively replace it.

To do this, we must understand the neurochemical con the Dopamine Cartel has pulled on us. They have trapped us in a cycle of seeking without ever finding. Dopamine is not the chemical of happiness; it is the molecule of *more*. It is the evolutionary driver that pushes us to seek out new information, but it never provides lasting contentment. Real-world fulfillment is governed by entirely different neurochemicals—specifically serotonin, which provides a deep sense of peace and satisfaction in the present moment, and oxytocin, which facilitates genuine human bonding. The digital world is engineered to hijack your dopamine pathways; the analog world is where you must go to harvest serotonin and oxytocin.

The Dopamine Cartel conditioned us to believe that effort is a design flaw. They sold us a reality where connection, entertainment, and validation are entirely frictionless. To rebuild your analog life, you must actively court friction. Real-world fulfillment is not immediate, and it is rarely easy. It requires patience, physical exertion, and a high tolerance for being temporarily bad at something. You must rediscover the profound satisfaction of tactile, high-friction hobbies.

Whether it is woodworking, cultivating a garden, knitting, learning a musical instrument, or mastering complex culinary techniques, these pursuits anchor you in the physical realm. When you build a piece of furniture or bake a loaf of bread, you are interacting with the uncompromising physics of the real world. You cannot swipe away a mistake. You cannot apply a digital filter to a poorly cut piece of wood or a burnt crust. The deep, lasting neurochemical reward comes precisely from the physical effort expended—a slow-release satisfaction that the fast-twitch dopamine of a social media feed can never replicate. You are trading the cheap illusion of digital influence for the quiet, unshakeable competence of physical mastery.

Beyond physical hobbies, you must actively rehabilitate your fractured cognitive hardware. The most potent antidote to the infinite scroll is the physical book. Deep reading is the exact neurological opposite of algorithmic consumption. A book demands your absolute, unbroken attention; it does not ping, vibrate, or shift its contents to cater to your waning focus. Initially, attempting to read a dense, physical book will feel agonizing. Your attention will fracture every few pages, and your hand will unconsciously twitch, searching for a device that is no longer in your pocket. You must push through this cognitive withdrawal. The act of holding a physical object, tracking linear arguments, and imagining complex narratives acts as vital physical therapy for your prefrontal cortex. It rebuilds the mental scaffolding destroyed by years of rapid context switching.

Furthermore, you must aggressively replace the hollow, metricized validation of the digital world with the messy, unquantifiable reality of human connection. The Matrix sold us parasocial voyeurism and called it "community." Real community does not exist in a comment section. It exists in shared physical spaces, marked by the nuances of body language, eye contact, and undivided presence. Reinvest the hours you previously spent managing your digital avatar into your physical relationships. Host a dinner party and enforce a strict no-phones policy. Join a local club, volunteer in your neighborhood, or simply take a walk with a friend without looking at a screen. Real-world relationships are inherently inefficient and often require navigating uncomfortable emotional terrain, but they are the only genuine cure for the profound social isolation the Cartel engineered.

Finally, you must re-inhabit your physical body. Years of living as a disembodied consciousness staring into a glass rectangle have severed our connection to our physical form. Engage in movement that requires pure presence—weightlifting, running, martial arts, or hiking. Leave the fitness trackers, the biometric watches, and the GPS mapping apps at home. Allow yourself to move through a physical environment without documenting it, tracking it, or optimizing it for a digital audience. Let your senses process the raw data of the real world: the temperature of the air, the unevenness of a dirt trail, the sound of an actual city instead of a curated digital playlist. Grounding your nervous system in physical reality is the ultimate defense against the artificial anxieties of the digital realm.

Escaping the Matrix is not ultimately a story of deprivation; it is a story of profound reclamation. You are not losing your digital life; you are getting your actual life back. When you replace the virtual hits with real-world fulfillment, you transition from a passive consumer of algorithmic content to the active author of your own existence. You build a deep reserve of self-worth and satisfaction that is entirely offline, immune to the shifting metrics of the Attention Economy, and finally your own.

Chapter 12: Life Beyond the Cartel

The preceding chapters have taken you through the darkest, most manipulative corridors of the Attention Economy. We have diagnosed the psychological, physical, and societal illnesses engineered by the Dopamine Cartel. We have mapped the invisible architecture of your digital captivity, and in the last chapter, we executed the tactical protocol required to sever the tethers. You have instituted the friction, set the boundaries, and endured the initial shock of cognitive withdrawal. You have successfully unplugged the machine. But escaping a prison is only the first half of the journey. The true challenge—and the ultimate triumph—lies in what you choose to build in the vast, open space of your reclaimed freedom.

Welcome to Chapter 12: Life Beyond the Cartel.

This final chapter is a blueprint for your permanent existence outside the Matrix. It is not enough to simply survive the digital detox; you must actively construct an analog reality so rich, so deeply fulfilling, that the hollow promises of the digital world lose their gravitational pull forever. We will begin this reconstruction at the neurological level in **Rewiring Your Brain for Sustained, Joyful Focus**. For years, your prefrontal cortex was held hostage by the frantic, fast-twitch rhythm of the infinite scroll. We will explore how neuroplasticity—the brain's miraculous ability to physically change and heal itself—allows you to fundamentally rebuild your attention span. You will discover that deep work and sustained focus are not just modern productivity hacks, but profound sources of intrinsic joy, quiet confidence, and intellectual mastery that the Cartel actively suppressed.

Next, we will address the most vital component of human existence in **Cultivating Deep and Authentic Real-World Connections**. The Matrix isolated you by offering a sterilized, metricized simulation of community. Now, you must return to the messy, unquantifiable, and beautiful reality of physical human bonding. We will guide you through the process of shedding the performative avatar you maintained online, teaching you how to forge relationships anchored in genuine vulnerability, shared physical presence, and undivided attention. You will learn that the true antidote to the profound loneliness of the digital age is not a wider network, but a deeper one.

Finally, we must navigate the practical reality of modern life in **Becoming a Conscious Consumer in a Digital Age**. Living beyond the Cartel does not require retreating to an isolated cabin or abandoning the conveniences of the twenty-first century. The internet, when stripped of its predatory algorithms and infinite loops, remains a powerful utility. We will establish the permanent framework for a healthy, entirely subordinate relationship with technology. You will learn how to interact with digital platforms strictly on your own terms, extracting exactly what you need without surrendering a single ounce of your behavioral data or emotional stability.

By the end of this chapter, the narrative of this book will close, but your autonomous life will begin. You will step forward not as a harvested commodity in a trillion-dollar ecosystem, but as a fully conscious, deeply grounded architect of your own time.

12.1 Rewiring Your Brain for Sustained, Joyful Focus

For years, the Dopamine Cartel operated on a terrifying assumption: that they could permanently break your attention span. And when you first step away from the Matrix, the cognitive damage can feel undeniably permanent. Your mind feels fractured, your patience is non-existent, and the mere thought of reading a dense physical book or sitting quietly with a complex problem for an hour induces a low-grade biological panic. You might easily conclude that your brain is irrevocably broken, reduced to a twitchy, hyper-reactive state incapable of the deep thought you once possessed. But this despair ignores one of the most miraculous biological realities of the human nervous system: neuroplasticity. The brain is not a static computer hard drive; it is a highly dynamic, living architecture. It constantly reshapes its own physical structure based on how it is used. The damage is entirely reversible, and the path to cognitive autonomy begins with actively rewiring your neural pathways for sustained, joyful focus.

To understand how to rebuild your attention span, we must understand the fundamental rule of neuroplasticity: "neurons that fire together, wire together." Every single time you felt a pang of boredom, anxiety, or cognitive friction and instantly reached for your smartphone, you reinforced a specific neural pathway. You essentially paved a massive, frictionless neurological superhighway linking "slight psychological discomfort" directly to "digital distraction." Over the years, this pathway became so thick and efficient that the behavior became an unconscious reflex. Reclaiming your focus requires starving this superhighway. You must systematically deny it the traffic it expects, while painstakingly clearing a new path through the overgrown jungle of your prefrontal cortex. You must force a new route that links "cognitive friction" directly to "sustained effort."

This rewiring process is not a passive healing period; it is active, grueling physical therapy for your brain, and it begins with an inescapable phase of intense discomfort. When you first sit down to engage in deep work—whether it is writing a complex document, studying a difficult text, or attempting to learn a challenging analog skill—your brain will inevitably rebel. Within five minutes, the cognitive friction will spike. Your hijacked limbic system, desperate for its accustomed algorithmic dopamine hit, will scream at you to check a feed, open a new browser tab, or find a vastly easier task. Most people interpret this sudden surge of anxiety and mental fatigue as a sign that they are simply incapable of focusing, and they surrender. But you must radically reframe this discomfort. This acute mental friction is not a sign of failure; it is the literal, biological sensation of your brain rewiring itself. It is the heavy lifting required to tear down the old pathways and forge the new ones.

You cannot rebuild this architecture overnight. If you attempt to force a completely atrophied attention span into a three-hour session of unbroken focus, your willpower will snap. You must treat your prefrontal cortex exactly like a physical muscle recovering from severe atrophy. You begin with progressive overload. Start by setting a timer for just fifteen minutes of absolute, uncompromising single-tasking. No digital tabs, no hidden phones, no ambient background interruptions. When the timer sounds, you stop. The next week, you push the boundary to twenty minutes, then thirty, then forty-five. As you consistently apply this progressive stress, a profound biological shift occurs within your skull. The neural pathways dedicated to sustained focus physically thicken and accelerate their transmission speeds. The persistent mental fog begins to lift. The agonizing urge to pull away from the work steadily diminishes, replaced by a growing, robust capacity to remain seated in the fire of difficulty.

As this neurological muscle strengthens, you will cross a critical, life-altering threshold: the transition from agonizing effort to profound joy. The Dopamine Cartel sold us the lie that effortless consumption is the peak of human happiness. In reality, effortless consumption only yields a fleeting, hollow chemical spike followed by an immediate, anxious crash. True, enduring human happiness is found in the "flow state." Flow is the psychological and neurological phenomenon that occurs when you are so deeply immersed in a challenging, meaningful task that your sense of time, your ego, and your awareness of external distractions completely dissolve. In this state, the brain is not flooded with the cheap dopamine of a slot machine; it is bathed in a complex, stabilizing cocktail of endorphins, anandamide, and serotonin.

The flow state is the Cartel's greatest enemy, because a human being locked in a state of joyful, sustained focus is completely un-monetizable. They are not viewing advertisements, they are not generating reactive data, and they are not looking for a digital pacifier.

This is the ultimate victory over the Matrix. Sustained focus ceases to be a grueling productivity hack and becomes an intrinsic source of deep, resonant joy. When your brain is successfully rewired for deep work, you discover a quiet, unshakeable confidence that comes from genuine mastery. You realize that you can tackle complex problems, build intricate skills, and engage with the physical world on a level of depth that the scrolling masses can barely comprehend. You are no longer skimming the shallow, agitated surface of your own intellect. You are diving into the quiet depths.

Reclaiming this capacity for deep work transforms your relationship with yourself, but it is only the foundation. A focused, autonomous mind is a powerful engine, but it requires a worthy destination. Once you have successfully rebuilt the architecture of your own attention, you must turn that newly restored focus outward. You must take the immense energy you have reclaimed from the digital ether and invest it in the only thing that genuinely sustains the human spirit. You must rebuild your capacity for real people.

12.2 Cultivating Deep and Authentic Real-World Connections

The most profound casualty of the Attention Economy is not our productivity; it is our biological capacity for genuine human connection. The Dopamine Cartel orchestrated a mass psychological bait-and-switch. They identified our deepest evolutionary drive—the need for tribal belonging—and sold us a sterile, metricized simulation in its place. We traded the messy, profound reality of physical community for the frictionless illusion of a digital network. We now possess thousands of "friends," "followers," and "connections," yet we are currently living through the most severe epidemic of mass loneliness in recorded human history.

To escape the Matrix, you must recognize that digital communication is a catastrophic downgrade in biological bandwidth. For millions of years, the human nervous system evolved to process social interaction through a highly complex, multi-sensory physical exchange. When you sit across from a human being, your brain is doing infinitely more than parsing their words. Your mirror neurons are firing as you subconsciously track their micro-expressions. You register the exact cadence and pitch of their voice, the dilation of their pupils, and their physical posture. This rich, high-fidelity data stream is what triggers the release of oxytocin, the neurochemical responsible for trust, empathy, and deep emotional bonding.

A text message, a comment, or an emoji contains absolutely none of this biological data. The digital interface strips away ninety percent of human communication and replaces it with a cold, low-resolution text string. When you rely on the Matrix for your social life, your limbic system essentially starves. It is the social equivalent of trying to survive on a diet of artificial sweeteners; it temporarily tricks the brain into thinking it is receiving nourishment, but the body remains profoundly malnourished.

Furthermore, the Matrix fundamentally warped our social behavior by introducing a digital buffer. Behind a screen, you control the narrative. You have the luxury of time to draft the perfect, witty response. You can apply a filter to your face and curate a highlight reel of your life to project an avatar of absolute perfection. But real-world human connection does not happen in the realm of perfection; it happens in the realm of vulnerability.

Because we have spent a decade communicating through this curated buffer, our analog social skills have severely atrophied. We have lost the tolerance for the natural friction of physical interaction. We panic during conversational lulls, unable to sit in comfortable silence. We avoid difficult, face-to-face conversations because the physical reality of seeing someone's disappointment or anger is too intense for a nervous system accustomed to simply swiping away from discomfort.

Cultivating authentic, real-world connection requires a deliberate, often uncomfortable process of rehabilitation. You must actively dismantle your digital avatar and re-enter the physical world without a shield.

The foundational step in this rehabilitation is the restoration of undivided physical presence. Attention is the currency of love. When you sit with a friend, a spouse, or a child, the smartphone cannot be on the table. It cannot be in your hand. As established in the previous chapter, the mere visible presence of a device signals to the other person that they are continually competing with the entire globe for your focus. To build deep connection, you must gift the person across from you the radical, uninterrupted focus of your newly rewired brain. You must look them in the eye and signal, biologically and psychologically, that in this specific moment, nowhere else matters.

Next, you must radically shift your objective from building a "wide" network to cultivating a "deep" community. The Matrix trained you to value the quantity of your social interactions over the quality. You must reverse this metric. Deep connection is not scalable. You do not have the emotional bandwidth to maintain genuine relationships with five hundred people. Identify the handful of individuals in your life who ground you, challenge you, and support you, and pour your reclaimed time and energy entirely into them.

Finally, you must actively court the messiness of uncurated existence. Invite people into your physical space, even when your house is not perfectly clean. Share the struggles, the anxieties, and the failures that you would never dare post on a digital feed. True intimacy is born precisely in the spaces where the polished avatar breaks down. When you allow someone to witness your unedited reality, and they offer empathy rather than judgment, the biological loop of genuine connection is completed.

Building a real-world community is inherently inefficient. It requires navigating scheduling conflicts, enduring awkward misunderstandings, and investing immense emotional labor. But this friction is the exact price of admission to a meaningful life. When you rebuild your physical tribe, you strip the Dopamine Cartel of its ultimate leverage. A human being anchored by the deep, unshakeable love of a physical community is entirely immune to the artificial isolation of the Matrix.

With your mind rewired and your community restored, you are finally ready to confront the last remaining challenge. You must learn how to re-enter the digital world without being consumed by it.

12.3 Becoming a Conscious Consumer in a Digital Age

The final frontier in the war against the Dopamine Cartel is not absolute exile; it is absolute sovereignty. When we first awaken to the staggering scale of algorithmic manipulation, the instinct is often to burn it all down—to discard the smartphone, sever the Wi-Fi, and retreat into an unyielding analog purism. But this reactionary stance grants the Cartel too much power. It operates on the false binary they created: either you surrender your entire mind to their ecosystem, or you forfeit the miraculous utility of modern human connectivity. The true victory does not lie in smashing the machine. True victory lies in subordinating it. You must transition from an algorithmic captive to a conscious, ruthless consumer of the digital age.

Becoming a conscious consumer requires fundamentally rewriting your economic and psychological relationship with technology. The most critical step in this transformation is abandoning the toxic illusion of "free."

For two decades, the internet has conditioned us to expect infinite software, global communication, and high-fidelity media at absolutely no monetary cost. We must finally accept the grim mathematics of this arrangement: if no money changes hands, the currency being traded is your behavioral data and your cognitive focus. To step outside the Matrix, you must begin actively paying for your digital existence. When you pay a transparent, monthly subscription for a secure email provider, a premium news outlet, or an independent search engine, a profound power shift occurs. You instantly transition from being the mined commodity to being the respected customer. The platform no longer needs to keep you endlessly engaged to serve you targeted ads; their only incentive is to provide a high-quality tool that solves your problem efficiently so you continue to renew your subscription. Paying for digital utility is the ultimate investment in your own psychological defense.

Once you have re-established a healthy economic boundary, you must fundamentally reverse the flow of information. The Dopamine Cartel relies entirely on a "push" dynamic. They push notifications to your lock screen, they push algorithmic recommendations into your feed, and they push auto-playing videos into your peripheral vision. The machine is designed to tap you on the shoulder every three minutes and tell you what to look at.

A conscious consumer operates strictly on a "pull" dynamic. You must strip your devices of all push capabilities. No red badges, no banners, no unprompted alerts. The device remains completely silent and inert until you decide you need it. You approach the digital world with a premeditated intention—a specific question to answer, a specific person to contact, or a specific route to navigate. You pull the exact information you require from the network, and the moment that transaction is complete, you sever the connection. You do not linger to see what the algorithm suggests next. You treat the internet like a sprawling, chaotic library: you go in to find a specific book, check it out, and leave. You do not stand in the lobby letting strangers scream random paragraphs at you.

This intentionality extends to how you participate in digital networks. Conscious consumption means recognizing that your attention is the most valuable asset you possess, and treating it with the corresponding paranoia it deserves. Before downloading a new application or signing up for a new service, you must run a strict cost-benefit analysis. You do not adopt a technology simply because it is ubiquitous or because your peers are using it. You ask yourself: **What precise friction in my physical life does this solve? Does the utility of this tool outweigh the behavioral data it demands? Will this application respect my time, or is it designed to harvest it?** If a piece of software cannot prove it is a subservient tool, it does not get installed.

Furthermore, becoming a conscious consumer means shifting your primary digital identity from a consumer to a creator. The Attention Economy thrives on passive absorption. It wants you slumped in a chair, endlessly scrolling through the labor and performance of others. To break the spell, use your remaining digital tools to actively build, write, design, and organize. Use the miraculous leverage of the internet to launch a project, coordinate a physical community event, or learn a complex analog skill. When you use the machine to create rather than consume, you hijack its power for your own advancement.

Ultimately, life beyond the Cartel is not a destination you arrive at; it is a permanent, daily practice of vigilance. The tech industry will not stop innovating. They will introduce augmented reality, immersive virtual ecosystems, and highly advanced artificial intelligence designed to mimic human empathy. The traps will become infinitely more sophisticated, subtle, and seductive.

But you are no longer blind to the architecture. You have audited your vulnerabilities, built your physical friction, rewired your prefrontal cortex, and anchored your soul in the unquantifiable beauty of the real world. You understand that the glowing screen is just glass, metal, and code. It possesses no inherent power over you. You are the architect of your attention. You are the sovereign of your own mind. And for the first time in a very long time, you are entirely, joyfully free.

www.ingramcontent.com/pod-product-compliance
Lightning Source LLC
LaVergne TN
LVHW071743071126
851857LV00045B/2075
* 9 7 8 9 6 9 9 3 9 8 4 5 2 *